T0157306

April 27, 2011
The Day My Life Changed

A True Testimony from Being a Victim to Being a Survivor

Stacy Landry

authorHOUSE®

AuthorHouse™
1663 Liberty Drive
Bloomington, IN 47403
www.authorhouse.com
Phone: 1-800-839-8640

Published by AuthorHouse 3/26/2013

ISBN: 978-1-4817-3480-6 (sc)
ISBN: 978-1-4817-3479-0 (hc)
ISBN: 978-1-4817-3478-3 (e)

Library of Congress Control Number: 2013905809

To my Father in Heaven and My Savior Jesus Christ for loving me unconditionally.

To my children, family and close friends that inspired me the most to write this book. They never gave up on me. To all the obstacles that came my way and forced me to move forward with a new beginning in life.

To my Church Family at Ashville First Baptist Church in Ashville, Alabama that took us under their wings and took care of us. The Love you showed and gave to my family and I was unconditional.

To all of you that built our home and spent many dedicated hours just to get us back home before Christmas. We love you all so much.

To Brother James Sampley and Sondra Yarbrough for never giving up Faith that God was going to provide a way for us all. For all the Prayers and love that you provided us when we had almost given up. We all love you so much.

To all the volunteers that dedicated so much of their time, came to our aid, and showed unconditional love to all of us in the Valley. We will never forget you and we love you, dearly. By showing how much you cared when you didn't even know us, you gave us Hope. You all showed us that we were not alone and what hurt us, also hurt you.

For all the loved ones that we lost on April 27, 2011 in Shoal Creek Valley. You are missed.

- Oberia Layton Ashley
- Ronnie Isbell
- Tammy Isbell
- Leah Isbell
- Bertha S. Kage
- Thomas Carl Lee
- Stella "Mae" Lovell
- Sandra Pledger
- Albert Sanders
- Angie Sanders
- Charlie Andrew Wolfe
- Nettie Ruth Wolfe

It was a typical Wednesday morning. The alarm clock buzzed at 4:45 a.m. It was time to get up already. It never seems like you get enough sleep. It felt as if I had only slept two hours. I needed at least five more hours of rest, I thought. I finally hit the snooze button. "Just five more minutes," I quietly said to myself. "Just five more minutes."

I finally got on up and went to make my morning coffee. I started throwing stuff together for my and my sons' lunches for work. I grabbed the last can of tuna fish and a pack of crackers for myself and made the usual lunches of ham sandwiches, chips, and snack cakes for my sons. As I quickly put everything into our lunch boxes, I kept looking over to see if the coffee had finished brewing.

Finally! The coffee was ready. I poured myself a cup and added my favorite coffee creamer—French Vanilla. "That's the stuff" as the kids would say. I took the first sip of coffee. *Oh my goodness! Now that's a good cup of coffee, I might add, even though it didn't come from a fancy coffee and doughnut shop.* Now I was ready to start the morning.

I looked outside the sliding glass door to see if it had started raining yet. The local weatherman had said the night before that we had a storm system approaching Alabama on Wednesday and for people to stay alert for any weather changes. The National Weather Service was stating that these storms were building and getting stronger, and we—that is the state of Alabama—were at high risk for severe weather.

However, when I looked outside, it was barely sprinkling. Thank goodness! I really wasn't looking forward to having to drive in the pouring rain at 6:00 a.m. in the morning. So I headed to my bedroom to get dressed for work so I could get out the door no later than 6:15 a.m. I kept thinking to myself that I sure could call into work and just stay home to keep an eye on the weather.

We had no weather alerts or warnings going off on the television or the weather radio so far, so I proceeded to get my son up for work and went and told my daughter that I was leaving. I said, “Ro’chele, I put your lunch money in your purse and your softball uniforms have been washed and dried and are sitting by your bag on the couch.” I kissed her little forehead and told her that I loved her and to have a good day. She nodded her little head yes, as if to tell me “okay.” At the time, my daughter was 16 years of age and both of my boys were 20 years old with two month difference between them.

I went into the living room and told my son one final time to get up for work. I told him that his lunch was on the kitchen counter by his wallet and truck keys and that I loved him. I wished him a good day and said that I was leaving for work. In reply, he said the same old thing: “*I’m up*!” So out the door I went.

I had gotten down to Bethany Baptist Church on Shoal Creek Road when the winds started picking up. As I got closer to the stop sign, I noticed some lightning back toward Highway 231. I remember saying to myself, “Oh Lord, here we go with the heavy rain.” But not for one moment would I have dreamed of what I am about to tell you.

I turned the radio up a little louder and started channel surfing for weather reports but found nothing. I continued seeking through channel after channel, but there were still no weather reports. I was beginning to get a little nervous, so I just found a radio station with music that I liked to keep my mind off of things so I could drive into work safely.

As I got closer to the end of Shoal Creek Valley, where Highway 231 intercedes, the winds picked up a little more. I made my normal left turn and headed south toward Pell City, Alabama. I usually took this route down 231 until I got to Highway 34 and then from there, headed toward Talladega. It was a slightly shorter route for me when I was working at the main plant. You see, I was a grade-IV wastewater operator and one of our plants was off the 275 Bypass. It was easier for me to take this route to work.

The rain started coming down pretty hard as I approached the first mountain on 231. We called this area Gulf Hollow mostly because it was such a drop-off, if you were to go off the side of this mountain, you probably would never be found. I was getting more nervous and a little anxious. I started channel surfing again and finally found a weather report. And guess what! St. Clair County—that was us—was under a severe thunderstorm warning with heavy rains, deadly lightning, and damaging winds up to sixty miles per hour predicted.

Then, all of a sudden, there it was, sitting on top of us as we all commuted into work. Trees were falling in front of me as well as behind me. The winds were unbelievable. The rain was coming down in heavy sheets, and I could barely see the road. I started praying, "God, lead me and direct me along with others to safety. Please keep my Chevy Impala on the road and not off the side of the mountain where I would never be found."

As I came down the first mountain and approached the second mountain, daylight was trying to break through the dark clouds, which made the skies look even angrier. All of a sudden, pine cones and small tree limbs were snapping and hitting both sides of my car. I looked up and out of my front windshield to see something that I had never seen before. Extremely tall and perfectly round pine trees were leaning completely over as their limbs from the tip-top of the trees touched the ground.

I started coming down the second mountain and saw that there were a few other cars in front of me as well. We were all driving slowly, and then we came to a complete stop. I started praying again. "Father, please help us all get out of here." I was by this time shaking badly; I trembled with fear for everyone who was traveling. I feared for my children and feared that I would never see them again.

Then I remembered that I had to call my son. He was getting ready to leave for work. I started praying again, "Lord, please let me have cell phone service." I looked at my phone and saw I had three service bars so I would be able to call out—or at least I was hoping that I could. Then I said, "Now, Lord, please let him, Lord ... please let my son still be at home."

I called the house, and a friend of mine answered the phone

instead of one of my children. You see, these friends had lost their home to foreclosure and I had opened my home up to them to stay with my family until they could find a new house. Her husband had been offered a job in Afghanistan, so he was not there at the time.

I had a lot of people tell me that I was a much bigger person than they were, that they just didn't know if they could do what I did to help this family. I would always reply with a response of: "It's been a challenge." I had often come home to hidden things, misplaced things, broken things, and even sometimes my private things having been gone through, but I always seemed to manage and never accused or showed my temper.

I kept telling people that I had done what I did to help them, as I was led by the good Lord above to do so. Everyone would tell me that they commended me and admired me for who I was and what I was doing for others. I would always say that I knew that good things would come about and many blessings. It may not be this lifetime, but God knew, and that was all that mattered.

She answered the phone, and I told her to give the phone to my son. She began asking questions. I frantically and firmly—for her to understand that this was not a time for the one-hundred-question talk—to give the phone to my son right then! He answered the phone with a "Hello?"

I said to myself, "Thank You, God, he is at home."

"Derrell," I said sharply. "Pay attention and listen to me. Do not—I repeat—*do not* leave the house. It's too dangerous. There are trees down everywhere on 231. You can't make it up through here. Do you understand me?"

He replied, "Are you okay? Where are you?"

I explained that I was okay. I told him that I was going to be all right and that I was at the second mountain on 231. He knew where I was because he drove that same route to work in Pell City every day as well. He was working on building the new hospital in town.

"Turn the weather on, Son. Talk to me!" I continued in a demanding voice. "What are they saying about the weather?"

There was a brief period of silence. I sensed concern from him, a feeling of discomfort. But then he replied, "It's almost past you."

I took a deep breath and calmly said, "Okay, baby." Then I

explained to him that no matter what not to try to go to work and not to let his sister leave for school. I told him that I didn't care if they had not canceled school; I was canceling school.

He said, "Yes, Momma."

"Derrell, watch the weather and watch it closely all day. Keep me informed if anything changes today. I will call you when I get to work to let you know that I made it all right. It may take me a little while to get to Talladega, but as soon as I get there, I will call you. I love you, Son." I hung the phone up, and I was back to dodging trees again.

I had another car in front of me, and we both had our emergency flashers on and were easing our way through the heavy rain, lightning, and strong winds until we got over the second mountain. Then, all of a sudden, we came to a complete stop because a huge tree had fallen across the highway. At this point on Highway 231, it was four lanes—two lanes going north and two lanes going south. So you can imagine how tall the tree was. It had covered the whole road.

I looked at my cell phone again to see if I had service or not so I could call my daddy. I still to this day don't think he understood what I was trying to say to him. He answered, "Hello?" in a very tired voice.

"Daddy," I said, "listen, I am on 231 at mile marker 223. I am trying to get to work, and we are stuck by trees down everywhere."

"I know," he said. "We have been out all night long working. Pell City is tore up pretty bad. We have got a lot of wind damage. Trees are down on some of the older houses up in town, and a lot of mobile homes have been destroyed. We have had a couple of fatalities from this morning's storm. Highway 34 has a lot of water on the roads, and trees are down over the roads there as well."

You see, my dad worked for the Street Department of Pell City. He had been with them for over thirty years. The guys who worked for him were family. They all stuck together. It didn't matter what time Daddy called them, they were always there and ready to do whatever they needed to do to get the city roads cleared and ready to be used. I told my dad that I would call him a little later and check in with him, I knew he was pretty busy, and I loved him.

I knew I had to try to get a hold of someone at work because it was already 6:30 a.m., and it was very obvious that I was not going to make it by 7:00 a.m. Max, my best friend and coworker, always got to work early, so I decided to call him and let him know what was going on. He could pass the word to Brian, our supervisor, for me.

Max answered with his usual, "Hey, baby."

"Max, listen, I'm stuck on Highway 231 because trees are down across both sides of the road, and I am on the mountain. I am going to be just a little late."

Max replied, "Are you okay? I heard that it got a little rough up your way from the storms."

"I am fine, Max, but I don't know how long it's going to take me to get into work. Could you pass the word on to Brian for me?"

"Yeah, baby, I'll let him know. You just be careful."

"Hey, Max, I'm going to take the interstate to Talladega as soon as I can get to it. Once I can get through to Highway 77, it shouldn't take me no time to get to work."

Max replied, "Okay, you just be careful and take all the time you need, and we will see you when you get here. If you have any more problems, just call me."

I said, "Okay, I will," and we hung up.

At this point, I kept telling myself, "It's going to be all right. We are all going to get out of this." Then I started praying again, "Father, help us. Please get us off this mountain." Approximately, fifteen minutes had passed, and another car had pulled up behind me. By this time, I had already turned my car off but left the flashers on. There was no sense in my car just sitting there idling and wasting gas.

It started feeling like it was going to be awhile before someone could get up through there to clear the roads for us. The longer I sat there, the more I started thinking. I said to myself, "I promise, I will never leave home again without seeing a complete weather report. Work will and can just wait. It's not worth losing your life over trying to rush into work to make it on time. It's not that important."

Then all of a sudden, I looked into my rearview mirror to see this Jeep Cherokee coming slowly around the car behind me. I kept looking through the mirror to see what he could possibly be trying to do. Then it hit me. I remember saying to myself, "Here is our way out and off this mountain. I just know it is."

See, I work with men, and it is wonderful. I love it. Being a hardheaded female, I have learned in the past fifteen-plus years of my life, that a man, at times, can be more sensible in making decisions. They do have a lot more patience than we women want to give them credit for. So I just knew deep down that this gentleman in this Jeep Cherokee was fixing to find us a way out of there.

I hit my brakes a couple of times to let him know to give me a minute. Then I cranked the car back up and moved over as much as I could, where he would have room to come around me. He slowly started coming around, and then the car I front of me moved over as well to let him in front. It started raining really hard again, but the gentleman in the Jeep got out anyway and was taking a look at the trees that had fallen across the road.

He walked through the branches and across to the other side. By this time, it was pouring. I knew he had to want off that mountain too, for him to be out in the rain getting soaked. I watched him patiently as he walked to the other side of the road looking to see how much room we had before we would go off the mountain and down in the hollow if we went around the tree. He stood there for a moment, studying the situation.

Then he got into his Jeep and slowly started moving toward the tree. He went over the first limb, which broke in half. Then he slowly went over the second limb, only for the first limb to pop up and hit his Jeep. Then he slowly went over the third and final limb. It crunched and broke as well. But he was through the tree, and that was all that mattered.

The car in front of me carefully moved in the direction of the tree, taking the same path as the Jeep. I followed slowly, as did the car behind me. We all made it through, and then we came up on another large tree that was across the road. We all proceeded to go through the same obstacle course, trying to get to safety and off that mountain. It was a slow go, but we made it through once again, thanks to the gentleman in the Jeep Cherokee.

I took a deep breath and gave a sigh of relief. Finally, I was home free—well, that was what I thought for a brief moment. When I looked to the left, I saw this huge old oak tree had fallen from someone's yard. It was not only blocking their driveway, but it was across 231 as well. I bet that tree had to be every bit of a hundred years old or older. It was the biggest one that I had seen yet that had been felled by the storms.

The good news was that we did at least have part of a driveway this time to attempt getting through this one. We were all desperate and just ready to get out of there. We didn't care at this point what we had to go through; we just wanted to get to safety. As I crossed over and through the limbs of this enormous tree, my Chevy Impala became a four-wheel-drive car. And Ford thought they were built tough. Hahaha. Have you met a Chevy lately?

I slowly moved over the limbs. I could hear them crunching underneath the car. I could hear branches scratching down both sides of my car as we went through too, but I didn't care. *Vehicles can be repainted or replaced and that is why I have Nationwide Insurance,* I thought to myself.

I just wanted to get out of there. We finally got through all the trees and started slowly down the mountain. We came to the bottom of Highway 231 into a small community called Coal City; we approached the head start school to discover that the road was completely shut down. You could not get through this tree. You could see yellow lights flashing and hear the sound of chainsaws from where people were trying to cut the tree and remove it limb by limb.

As I got closer to the other cars, I started looking for another driveway that I might possibly turn around in. I knew this area. There was another little side road that I could chance going down. I mean, what was it going to hurt? As I got turned around, I looked in my mirror to see that a few people had decided to do the same thing.

I started looking around as I was going down the road to see if there was damage. But believe it or not, it wasn't that bad. There were pine cones everywhere from the winds and a few limbs down but no trees. I didn't see any damage to homes, thank goodness. After what I had just gone through, I was very happy to see no damage or fallen trees on houses.

I had to stop at this little store before I got back on Highway 231. I kept hearing a noise coming from underneath my car. It sounded like I was dragging a tree branch. I got out and took a look under my car, and sure enough, I had not one but several limbs stuck underneath the car. I was able to reach one and remove it, but the others I couldn't reach with my short arms. I got back in the car. I had already decided that—I hoped—as I was driving, they would turn loose, and if not, I would get the guys at work to help me out.

I got back on 231 and called work to let Brian know where I was and that I was finally—or at least I hoped—in the clear. I was on my way and would call him if I ran into any more problems. As I got closer to Pell City, I never thought I would be so happy to see a Walmart in my life. I knew I was closer to the interstate, and I was thinking, *Finally, I might can get to work.*

There was a lot of debris on the interstate as well—anything from pine needles to pine cones and small tree branches. When I came up on Riverside, Alabama, I started looking around and saw where they had had some damage as well. The whole county of St. Clair ended up with some type of wind damage to their property and homes.

I had talked with my mom earlier, right before I had gotten on the interstate, and she had informed me that the news stated there was a lot of damage. I'd had to cut our conversation short because my focus was on driving. I had told her that I would call her after I got to work and I would also call my sister to let her know that I had made it okay.

I called the kids once I had gotten on Highway 77 to check in on them. My daughter answered the phone this time, and I asked her if we had any trees down or damage to the house, and she said we didn't. She told me that she and her brother had walked around the house and didn't see anything wrong. I told her that was good and I was getting closer to work.

I also warned them to make sure they kept a close eye on the weather because of the predictions that they had for us in the forecasts. She agreed and told me that she thought Derrell was going to have to go into work. I told her that I figured once they got the roads cleared that he would, and we hung up the phone.

As I got closer to the main plant, I decided to call a close friend of mine to check on his mother and daddy because they lived in Pell City. I am not going to disclose any names for personal reasons, but I will tell you that we grew up together. He was a very close friend and would always be dear to my heart. He was a very sincere and caring person.

He had always been very careful about who he showed his true feelings to. After we both graduated from high school, we went our separate ways. I guess it had been twenty-plus years since we had seen each other. But I had always kept him in my heart. He was always there for me when I needed a friend. He even taught me how—well, I will say, he *tried* to teach me how—to drive a straight-shift Mustang. That was a hilarious moment. Back in the day, the good ol' innocent days.

I had always kept something he said to me one night very close to my heart. We were sitting on the bank of the river, and he casually said, "You see that star?" I said I did in a puzzled tone of voice. Then he pointed to another star in a different direction and said, "You see that star over there? Well, those two stars are going to meet before the night is over." Sometimes I find myself still waiting for them to meet.

We had traveled down separate roads and had different responsibilities that consumed us in completely different directions. But I knew would always care about him. He was probably my soul mate, but as we all know, things happen for a reason. We just can't explain those situations sometimes, much less understand them.

When I talked with him, I asked him if he had talked with his mom and dad because it had gotten pretty rough in Pell City. He said he had talked with his dad and that they were all okay. They didn't have any damage. I told him that I just wanted to check on them, that I was almost at work finally, and I needed a cup of coffee. I told him it had been a challenge for me to get to work. He asked me if I was okay and I made our conversation short and said that everything was fine. I wasn't about to give him any indication that I was a nervous wreck. But I was finally at work and that was all that mattered.

Max met me outside as I drove up to the plant. I got out of my car, and he examined it for damage. I calmly looked at him, took a deep breath, and said, "I made it! Now I need a cup of coffee."

Max replied, "There is some waiting on you." I went into the building, poured myself a cup of coffee, and sat down a moment to gather myself to where I could think and function once again. After about twenty minutes, I was able to get up and do my job. My mind was clear, and the anxiety had passed. I made all my phone calls to let everyone know that I had made it to work and that I was okay.

The air just didn't feel right all day long. I just had this strange feeling inside. Something just did not feel proper. But I had no idea what the day had laid out for any of us. We all watched the weather closely all day. I was just glad that the bad weather predictions were for later in the afternoon to evening hours. The majority of the people would—I hoped—get home safely before the storms hit.

It was 2:45 p.m., and we were all getting ready to leave the plant and go home. I told everyone to keep a close eye on the weather and to stay safe. They all replied, "You too. You have a little further of a drive than we do."

We all got into our vehicles and left for home. Needless to say, none of us knew that this would be our last hugs and good-byes at work together as a family.

As I was commuting my regular route home, I observed the damage from that morning's storms. There was a lot of tree damage everywhere, and as you looked further off the side roads on 34, you could see the homes that had been damaged. Some still had trees laid over on top of their roofs. I felt bad for the homeowners, as they were waiting on help and insurance adjusters to come out.

It was very sad to see these people wondering whom to call for help. What were they going to do before the next storm, and where were they going to stay? I had tears in my eyes. I felt so bad for them. Even though I had no idea of what they were feeling or what could possibly be going through their minds, I felt so much sorrow for them.

As I headed North on Highway 231 toward Ashville, I could see where people had cut up trees that were down—even the trees that had fallen across the roads earlier that morning. You could see the damaged mobile homes on the mountain where we were stuck earlier that morning. All I could say to myself was that I hoped that we didn't have any more storms. I was hoping that the weatherman would be wrong about his weather predictions for later that evening. I turned onto Shoal Creek Valley Road headed home. I began to look around our valley for any damage. We were very blessed that we had none from the morning storms.

When I got home from work, I washed up and changed clothes. My daughter was so exhausted between softball practice, softball games, and keeping up with her schoolwork and grades that she had fallen asleep in her bed reading. So I just left her to sleep for a while.

I went to the kitchen and fixed myself a cup of coffee and then went to figure out what to cook for supper. Broiled chicken with salt and pepper and sautéed onions and green bell peppers sure did sound good. The fixings would be cream potatoes, mac and cheese, corn, and rolls. It was a pretty simple supper, and it sure would not take long to cook. So I got busy cooking. I wanted to get through with dinner before the news came on just in case the weather did turn out pretty bad as predicted.

For some reason, all day at work, I just kept having this weird feeling—you know, one of those gut feelings that you really can't explain—like I knew something was wrong but I just didn't know what it was. It just didn't feel right. Both of my boys had gone into work later that morning after the storms had passed, but something just simply did not feel right.

I got supper cooking and decided to walk out onto the porch for a minute. The air just had this strange and really unexplainable feeling to it. I went back inside to finish cooking supper. I called my son Derrell on his cell phone and asked him how much longer he was going to be at work. He told me that he was on his way home as we were speaking. I asked him if he had talked to Chase, my other son, and he said, "Yes, Momma, and he is on his way home too." I told him that was good and to be careful and hurry home as soon as he could.

Now before anyone gets confused, let me explain about Chase.

Chase is my other son. He is not my biological child, but that doesn't matter. Chase and Derrell were two months apart in age, and they had been best friends since youth league baseball. He had lived with us for a long time, and we had all taken care of one another. He called me Mom and referred to Derrell and Ro'chele as his brother and sister. I wouldn't have had it any other way.

Derrell was working for a construction company, and Chase was part-time with the Air National Guard and also working for a tile company. I was very proud of both of my boys. They were staying out of trouble, holding down steady jobs, and making something out of their lives. I was also so proud of my daughter, doing all that she did while making sure she got an education. God blessed me with three wonderful children. We were all very close. We always took time for one another and spent quality family time together. I couldn't have asked for anything more.

I was finishing up supper when both of the boys got home from work. Ro'chele was still sleeping. The boys went ahead and got their showers while I finished up. By that time, the evening news was about to come on. We all sat down in the living room glued to the television. We didn't even fix our dinner plates because of the headlines about the possibility of tornado outbreaks. Then, all of a sudden, the news went from regular programming straight to the weather.

The first thing they said was, "You know we have been watching the weather pattern closely all day forming over the state of Mississippi. Mississippi has been pounded all day long with some area damage, and it is crossing over the Alabama line. This is a significant weather pattern that has increased in size and has gotten not only bigger but stronger as well. Everyone needs to pay close attention to the weather the next several hours. These storms are developing stronger with the high possibility of major tornado outbreaks across the whole state of Alabama. We are sorry for interrupting the normal news programming, but the weather is our main concern at this time."

Something told me then that this was going to be a very long night. The phone rang, and it was my dad telling me to keep an eye on the weather because it might get rough on us. Boy, was he so correct. The boys and I watched eagerly as the storms approached Tuscaloosa, Alabama. The next thing we knew, the meteorologist was going back and forth from radar to radar.

They started putting out warnings all over Tuscaloosa, Alabama, telling the people to take cover. The storm was producing large hail, damaging winds, and cloud-to-ground-lightning along with tornadoes. Then we heard the meteorologist come back with this statement:

"This storm is huge. It's at least a mile to a mile and a half wide. Please, everyone, pay close attention as this system is approaching. It is very dangerous. If you are on the interstate, take cover now. If you plan on traveling anywhere, change your plans. Consider staying at home or wherever you are at the moment. It is not safe. This storm is no joke, people. Please pay attention."

Then they started projecting the paths that it would take and the times it would reach the locations. We had storm chasers everywhere. They were even trying to get ahead of the storm to the projected areas expected to be affected as well. As the storm got closer, there were more and more concerns about the damage that it could possibly cause.

All of a sudden, the meteorologists were running back and forth like crazy. It wasn't just one storm. They were popping up everywhere. I actually felt sorry for them because they were having to do coverage on back-to-back counties spread out over the whole state of Alabama. I have to say, they got their payday earned very well that day.

They would broadcast and warn people in one area to turn around and have to warn another area. At times, one weatherman would be at the radar and the other at the computer systems, and they were talking back and forth making sure that the other would get all the updated information that needed to get out to the people.

As it got closer to downtown Tuscaloosa, they started warning people on Mcfarland Boulevard and the University of Alabama campus. I remember I kept thinking to myself that this just couldn't be possibly happening. They were telling everyone in those areas to take cover and quickly. The weather sirens were going off like crazy, and you could hear them in the background as the meteorologists were telling people of the location and prediction of the path of the tornado.

They started having reports of vehicles being overturned on Interstate 20. They went to their web cameras, which they had out in certain areas of Tuscaloosa. Some areas that they showed were not even getting rain. It was so strange. Then they showed Mcfarland Boulevard, and there she was—this huge storm system getting ready to sit down on Tuscaloosa. Absolutely unbelievable.

There was complete silence in the living room as we sat there and watched this huge, amazing storm. They started showing pictures of what they called a "debris ball" from the tornado. We were all speechless. We had never seen anything like it before. One of the web cameras picked up the tornado as it was touching down on Mcfarland Boulevard, destroying everything in its path.

The meteorologists stood in amazement and shock, as the strength and size of this tornado as it was taking its path was just so unbelievable. The only thing anyone could do was sit in silence and pray that everyone had gotten into some type of shelter or safe place and that no one would be killed. It was very heart-wrenching and devastating to watch as people's lives were being turned upside down. The tornado was so massive that the last thing any of us thought was how could anyone possibly have survived such destruction. "Please God," I said silently, "help those people. Please be with them and take care of them."

The meteorologists were just standing there waiting for someone to call in with reports of the damage. As silence came upon everyone and they patiently waited on any reports, they had to start coverage on other areas that were in the path of this storm and also other storms that were coming about. We were having tornado outbreaks everywhere.

At first, they thought that the tornado had picked up from the ground and had lost strength, but that wasn't the case by any means. Sad to say, it had grown in size and in strength. It was going to destroy anything in its path. It only seemed like forty seconds and parts of Tuscaloosa were gone. The tornado just kept going.

There were just tornadoes after tornadoes. One was predicted toward Bessemer, Alabama, and it was headed straight for those people. I told my two boys then to go quickly and check in with our good friend and neighbor and take a look at the shelter he had. I told them to get him and make sure there weren't any snakes, spiders, or water down in the shelter. I said, "This storm system is no joke and definitely not playing." I warned them to hurry up because time was essential. They both hurried out the door, jumped in Derrell's truck, and took off.

Meanwhile, I sat there in a daze, staring at the television and the reports that were coming in. I guess I was hoping that all of this was just a bad dream and that I would wake up at any given time. But in reality, that wasn't the case. As I steadily watched the news, I began replaying tornado safety rules in my head—what to do, where to go, what to bring. My mind was just going ninety to nothing.

With the type of work that I had done for the past fifteen years, we had to take some type of safety class every year—anything from spider bites to chlorine leaks, natural disasters, and weather safety. I was hoping there was something that I had learned that I could refer back to and use. I got up and started pacing the floors. I walked outside and looked up at the sky to see what the clouds looked like. I could feel it in the air. Something just wasn't right. The humidity had risen up drastically. The air was tight feeling like there wasn't any oxygen.

The boys returned home from our neighbor's house after checking into the shelter and making sure everything was okay. They said, "Mom, it looks good. We are ready." I took a deep breath and sat back down in the living room to focus on the weather. I started getting a little nervous because the storm was working its way up through the 280 Bypass area in Jefferson County.

I can still hear, to this day, the meteorologist's words: "Please, everyone, if you're just tuning in, pay close attention to what I am saying. This storm is massive. Everyone needs to get to and in their place of safety now." One good thing was that most school systems either didn't open from the morning storms that had come through or closed early so all the kids and faculty could get home safely before the storms. Even a lot of local businesses had already closed to let their employees get home. When this happens, you know something serious is coming.

I was sitting there with my hands together, twirling my thumbs in a circle, like it was helping me think or something. Just another sign of nervousness. We often had storms in the past, and we would all go to my neighbor's house for the storms always to go in the opposite direction—which was good, don't get me wrong. But I started remembering what the kids would often say: "See, we left for no reason."

This time, though, something was different. Something just didn't feel right. The meteorologists started predicting the possible projected areas for the path of this mile- to mile-and-a-half-wide tornado. They were predicting the Clay, Chalkville, and Trussville, Alabama, areas. I looked at the boys and said, "It's time. Let's get ready to leave. Derrell, go get your sister up. Make sure she gets her tennis shoes on and grabs her a pillow and blanket. Chase, get us some water and Gatorade together and go throw it in the truck."

As I was rounding everyone up, including the people living with us, Ro'chele came stumbling half asleep into the kitchen and her brother was coming out of the bedroom with hard hats in his hands.

I began chuckling at them. What a team the three of them made. I was so proud of my boys and how well they took care of their baby sister. Sometimes they were a little overprotective, but that was okay. I knew that whatever the circumstance, they would always take good care of her. I believed that the three of them would always stand beside each other and always just be a phone call away when they all grew up.

They would always have their sibling spells of disagreement with one another, but that didn't mean that they wouldn't figure things out together, which was absolutely wonderful. Most siblings ended up in fist fights. One thing about them was you didn't mess with their family. If you did, they would be tag teaming up and coming for you. I do have to say, watching them take care of one another was about the cutest thing I had ever seen.

God blessed me beyond measurement when He gave me my children. We made the perfect pair in my eyes. We always had a way to fix our problems together, and we definitely took time for each other. I thanked my Father in Heaven every day for trusting me with these children that he so blessed me with. My life would not be complete without them. I might be a single parent and often wished for a true companion, but at the same time, that hole was filled with the joy of my little family.

I had been divorced for twelve years, and out of those twelve years, I had my challenges being single. But God always had a plan. Often, it was a plan that I never completely understood and more than likely never would. I always knew that my Father in Heaven had a plan to mold me and make me a better person for the near future, but some of the challenges that I had endured in my life, in the past and present, I would never have dreamed of having to face.

I sprinted off to my bedroom and grabbed my purse and work boots. I then went back into the kitchen and proceeded to throw some peanut butter crackers into my purse. About that time, Ro'chele said to me, "You need your running shoes instead of your work boots." I just smiled at her. Then I happened to look over my shoulder to see that the lady who was living with us was fixing herself a plate of food that I had cooked for supper. Then it dawned on me that she was not taking me seriously about this weather even after she had sat there and watched it with us.

I was furious. I turned around and told her in a sharp tone, "We don't have time to eat. We have to get out of this house!" She continued to shovel food down in her mouth, and I ordered her to get her daughter and herself into the car because we had to leave now! I told her sharply, "You should have eaten earlier after I got through cooking if you were that hungry. You had plenty of time." I didn't mean to be so ugly, but she had—or at least she acted like she had—problems understanding things sometimes.

I don't even remember if I turned the coffeepot or even the oven off. At that moment, that was the least of my worries. I just knew that I had to get my family and the others who were staying with us out of that trailer and to safety somewhere and fast. This system was coming quickly, and no one really knew which direction it might possibly turn.

As I got everyone out the door, I made the decision for us to take Derrell's brand-new silver Dodge truck that he had not even had three months yet and Ro'chele's red Toyota 4Runner. We had to leave everything else behind. The winds started picking up tremendously, and I figured that if trees started falling down, we could get over them in the trucks a lot better than in my car. My car had gone through enough from the morning storms that I'd had to take it through.

We all walked out to the vehicles. I stood there to watch the boys get in the truck. I looked around a brief moment, walked to my daughter's 4Runner, and opened the passenger door to get in. The daughter of the other lady was sitting there. I politely told her that she was going to have to get in the backseat with her mother. She looked at me with this surprised look on her face.

When she got out, she made this huffing noise under her breath at me muttering about who did I think I was. I told her that I had to be up front where we could get through any obstacles that we might be faced with. Lord knew she couldn't make proper decisions.

The winds had picked up even more as we started to leave. When we started up the driveway, shingles off houses were flying everywhere. Whether they were from our house or someone else's, we were not sure and still are not to this day. This storm was so massive and so strong it could have possibly been debris from somewhere else that we were seeing flying through the air. I just knew we had to hurry and get down to our neighbor's house.

The winds were so strong that they were pushing our vehicles from side to side as we went down Shoal Creek Valley. We didn't even have to go a mile, and it was still a challenge. We finally conquered the winds and pulled up in the driveway. It looked like over half the neighbors in the valley were standing on his back porch. A total of seventeen of us were there.

We all said our normal hellos and how-have-you-been. All of us there were the usual group of friends who, for the past twenty years, had always come down when we had strong storms with the possibility of tornadoes. It was just something that we all—or should

I say most of us—had always done. I guess we all knew that we would be safe and would always take care of each other.

Before I go any further, I just want to say this. There was a reason that all of us ended up together down at the house like we did. None of us regret it, and none of us ever will. God had a plan, and we didn't know it. That is pretty amazing and powerful, and you're fixing to understand why I say this. God wanted us all together. He knew we would take care of one another no matter what the situation might bc.

As we all gathered on the porch, it started raining pretty hard. They had the weather on the local television station, and one of the husbands would come out to update us on everything—where the storm was and the path they were saying it was going to take, whether it was headed our way or if it was going to turn and go the opposite direction.

My neighbor's back porch was very nice. It went from one end of the house to the other. He had rocking chairs and a swing on the porch. We all had plenty of room to sit and gather beside one another. He had built his home himself a few years back. It wasn't a log cabin home, but one of those very nice, I guess you could say like a timber home. It was gorgeous, absolutely beautiful. He built it the way he wanted it. He took his time building, but he built it from his heart and the way he dreamed of it.

He had an outdoor brick fireplace and grill in an area that he chose by some trees. With the scenery, it was as if you had opened up a home-and-garden book—one of those homes that most people only dream of having. Well, he put his dreams together. He had a greenhouse and a carpenter's shop where he enjoyed building things from wood. I actually had one of the cedar trunks that he had built. I kept all of the kids' baby things in it. He built birdhouses and rocking chairs too. You name it, he could build it. It was his hobby and kept him busy.

He had even built a deck leading to his above-ground pool, which ran from the back porch. What a dream home! But, like I said, he was very creative. He also had a pond that he built and put catfish in. In the front, he had pear trees that lined up in the front of the house.

In the spring, when they bloomed, it just really made his house stand out with beauty.

He was a true old-time farmer. He had his hay fields, which he tended to. He had cattle, horses, donkeys, and a vegetable garden that he was proud of. He was always a hard worker and farmer. He was one of those people who would do anything for you, if he could. He would always bring you vegetables when he had extra from his garden. He was a very good friend to all.

We were all still gathered together on the back porch, and as I said earlier, it began raining very hard. Then it started hailing. The hail was the size of nickels and was coming down like rain. I had never seen such before. We all had made the comment that we hoped everyone had good auto insurance because of the damage the hail was doing to the vehicles. Then we all kind of laughed about it. I mean seriously, you can't do a whole lot about hail damage.

Then the next weather report came on, and it was showing that the storms were in Argo, Alabama, which wasn't too awfully far from us. The next area to be warned was Odenville and up Highway 411 and then up Highway 231 North. It was thought that the storm was going to travel up the side of Ashville High School. Don't get me wrong; I didn't wish anything on anyone, but at that point, we were all relieved that it was staying north of our community. At least, that was what we thought.

We figured that we would get the backside of the storm with heavy rain, hail, lightning, and some winds—maybe a few tree limbs down but nothing serious. As I said before, God had a huge, amazing, and powerful plan that no one would be able to comprehend at that time, much less be able to explain then or later.

Some of us were sitting, and others were standing, when all of a sudden, the storm seemed to be calming down for a minute and moving on from us. Were we fooled! We started having cloud-to-ground lightning like I had never seen in my entire life. When it hit, it was so powerful that it even made the phone ring. When that happened, all of our mouths dropped open in shock. I know, crazy. But it happened. Then we lost the satellite signal, which was our only source for the local weather updates. This was one disadvantage of living in the country; we had no underground cable, only satellite. We had no time to search for a radio before we had lost complete power.

The air started feeling tight again. It was like something was taking away the oxygen. We had another strong cloud-to-ground lightning bolt strike very close to the porch this time. We were already getting all the children into the house. There were children from the age of two years old up to the age of nineteen with us.

The adults started going into the house after all of the children were inside. A dear friend of mine was holding open the outside screen door for everyone to get inside. I stopped in front of her to hold the door open for her to go on inside, and as I was going to go in after her, I just completely froze in my tracks. There it was. I looked up above her head into the sky, and there was this huge black as black could be thing coming straight toward us. My mouth had dropped. At that time, I didn't know that this thing was an EF4 tornado.

I will never forget the little dance that she did. She saw the look on my face as my eyes looked down at her, and she did this little two-step jingle of a dance as if to say, "Oh my gosh!" as she had seen my facial expression. I started yelling for everyone to get in the house and get in there now. I looked around to see who was left on the porch and was screaming at everyone at the same time.

A lot of us were in the living room for a brief moment. Then all of a sudden, it started getting darker and darker in the house. Everyone scattered everywhere, trying to find some place to get into for shelter. We were all trying to hide under something that might protect us a little from this massive storm that was fixing to have a direct hit on us.

I was, at the time, beside my daughter. I had no idea at the moment where my boys were in the house. I got behind her and started pushing her and screaming at her to get toward the bathroom. She started screaming back at me to stop pushing her. I finally got her shoved into the bathroom. I know she didn't understand at the time why I was being so aggressive pushing her into the bathroom. I felt very bad for having to do it and be so rough with her, but I did what I had to do, for her safety.

There were people in the hallway, just wherever they could get away from windows as much as possible. I didn't know this at the time, but one of my sons, Derrell, ended up in the kitchen and living room area when the tornado hit. My other son, Chase, was coming up the hallway with a mattress to try to cover up as many people as possible in the hallway.

I must warn you that the rest of this is going to be pretty horrific and graphic. But at the same time, you must remember that this is a true story of actual events. Some of you may cry, while others will want to know how to express feelings of amazement. These things actually happened and to this day are still horrifying. I know in the back of my mind that I still question the possibility of it ever happening again. Some people have said that it will never happen again. But you know as well as I do that you can't predict weather just like you can't predict people and their behaviors.

I remember hearing, as we were in the bathroom, this loud roaring noise that I had never heard before. Some people would describe it as what you would hear if you were sitting on top of a large locomotive train. I have even heard people say that it sounded like a woman screaming. But to me, it was indescribable. I just know that it is a sound that I will never forget.

I remember my ears popping and then clogging up from the pressure. There was no oxygen in the air. It was very difficult to breathe. It was so dark that I could hardly see anything in front of me. The house started shaking like an earthquake was coming through. I guess I knew in the back of my mind that this tornado was coming into the house with us.

My daughter and I were standing in front of the bathroom vanity. Her brother had put one of the hard hats on her head when we were on the porch. I took the left side of my hip and moved my daughter over and out of in front of the vanity. I knew I had to get her moved back because she was so small, the cabinets from the vanity would have killed her on impact. I had a little more cushion on my body to handle it than she. Like I said from the beginning, my children are my life. I took my left arm and pulled her head down to her knees the best that I could and held on to her as much as I could. I remember saying to myself, "Here we go. And there isn't anything we can do about it."

The next thing I knew, the vanity was coming in on me, and the pressure from this thing was so incredibly powerful, it is beyond description. The last thing that I actually remember seeing was the wall coming in on us. The bathroom mirror fell toward me, and then the vanity was shoved into my stomach. It was like a bulldozer coming into the house straight for us. And then the roof was being peeled off, and the house basically blew out and exploded. My daughter had been completely ripped out of my arms and taken away from me.

The next thing I knew, I was facedown, lying on my stomach about a hundred and fifty yards from where the house used to be in the field. I remember trying to get up on my knees only to be knocked back down. I had been hit so hard in the back by debris that not only did it knock the breath out of me so badly that I was gasping for air, but the pain was so bad that I pray that I never feel such pain ever again. It was such a blunt, strong direct hit to my back that it actually numbed me. Whatever hit me knocked me flat back on my face. It was so bad that I asked God to please kill me.

I attempted a second time to get up to be knocked back down again with debris continuously hitting me. This time, the pain was not as bad because my body was still numb from the first hit. I again asked God to please kill me, as I was being pushed back down on my face. You know, I'd had people tell me all the time that I was very hardheaded. I have to admit, I actually agree with them because I attempted for a third time to get up, all to be knocked down on my face again. I remember gasping for air and asking God to just please kill me. "Why won't you just kill me?"

As I lay facedown in the dirt and grass, I decided to stay down and try to turn my head to the right of me. As I did, I was able to see the backside of the tornado moving away from us. It was this gray and white cloud swirling around fiercely. As I watched it move on past us, I decided I would attempt to get up. I had to find my children.

Before I go any further, we all have been told that the brain is a very powerful thing. It knows things before you even really recognize them. Well, when I started getting up again, for some odd reason, I was getting up with my left arm. I managed to get up on my knees and proceeded to push up with my left arm and get into a standing position. For some reason, I automatically took my right arm into my left and held it to my stomach, not daring to move it.

I began looking around. I saw such a horrific sight. I was getting anxious, and my heart started beating so fast. I began thinking, *Oh Lord, help us! My children, where are my children? Oh my gosh, no! Please don't let them be dead.* As I began looking around again in so much shock, I noticed that everyone had been thrown in a perfect circle like we were supposed to stay together during the storm and after.

I tried to scream for my children, but I couldn't get anything out. I call this a silent cry. I tried twice, and I just couldn't get any sound out of my voice. I finally screamed again, but this time, my daughter's name came out. In a panicked tone, I cried, "Ro'chele!" I had tears running down my face as I continued screaming, "Ro'chele! Ro'chele, where are you?"

Then all of a sudden, out of nowhere, on the far northeast of my left side, my son Derrell popped up off the ground and out of the debris. He looked around in astonishment. He shook his head as if to try to recognize where he was and what he was doing. I looked at him and started screaming again in a frantic voice. I was gasping for air and said, "I can't Find Ro'chele. We gotta find your sister." About that time, my other son Chase popped out from under some debris.

The worst feeling a mother could ever have is the feeling of losing her children. I absolutely couldn't find her, and I in feared that she was dead after seeing the devastation around me. I was going insane trying to find her. I started sweating in fear. My heart was racing, and all I could do was stand there in shock, looking around and screaming.

I saw the boys take off running. They had found her. She must have heard my screaming for her because she raised her little arm up out from underneath debris that had her pinned to the ground. They swooped her up and in just time. She couldn't breathe under all the rubble on top of her. Her pants were down to her ankles, and they pulled them up for her. Somehow, her cell phone had survived and still was in her pocket. We were all in such shock that we were not aware of our injuries at that moment.

The boys automatically started searching for everyone else, attempting to do a head count to make sure everyone was there and that no one was missing. As I began looking around again, I was still in complete astonishment that this tornado had spit us all out in a circle, and we were all still together. Like I said before, God had a reason and a plan for why we were all together. Yes, we do have a purpose in life. That purpose is for God.

The winds started howling like crazy again. I guess it scared Derrell so bad that he ran over to his sister, grabbed her up, and ran with her over to the backside of one of the vehicles that was actually still there. Then he yelled for me to get over there as well. We leaned up against the truck for a moment and then started looking around again.

Derrell looked over and saw Ro'chele's Toyota 4Runner down close by the pond. He took off running for it and jumped in it. I could not believe that it actually cranked, but it did. He attempted to try to move it closer to us, but it kept getting stuck. We had so much rain that the ground was soggy. Derrell's truck was nowhere to be found. We had no idea where it was at the time. He continued spinning in the 4Runner until he got it unstuck and moved from where the tornado had pushed it down by the pond.

Derrell got it on up by where we were. He was going to sit Ro'chele down in the seat; she started crying and holding her head because it hurt so badly. But there was glass everywhere—in the seats and floorboard, just everywhere in the 4Runner. She just kept crying that her head hurt. She had a piece of glass about two inches long stuck in her forehead and a huge knot on the back of her head along with a deep cut about six inches long where something had cut her pretty badly. It ran from the top side of her head on the right side down to her lower neck area. She reached up to her forehead and pulled the piece of glass out of her head hoping to stop some of the pain.

Derrell got her sat down and told her just to stay there and not to move. He left her to go help others. Chase and Derrell were going person to person accounting for everyone, seeing what injuries people had, and trying to help them the best way that they knew how. Both boys had had training as first responders a few years back, and Chase had training from the Air National Guard as well.

The timing of the tornado was exactly 6:23 p.m. I watched the boys working hard, helping people. There were so many bad and serious injuries. It was like the worst nightmare that anyone could ever have. The boys had to pick up a transformer pole off of one person.

I heard someone yell out my name. "Stacy! Stacy, help me! I can't find my son!" It was my other neighbor's grandson calling out to me. As I started limping toward him, I once again made sure my arm wasn't moving out of the position that I had put it in earlier. I didn't think he was alive because he was so little. Someone found him. I am not sure who. But he was going to be okay. He had cuts everywhere, and his little leg was injured, but he was alive and responsive.

I fell down on my knees beside my neighbor who I didn't think was alive. It was his grandson who had yelled out to me. I nervously and frantically started calling out his name. I kept telling him to talk to me in a very demanding voice. "Do something to show me you're alive!" I screamed out his name once again to try to get him to respond to me. I didn't want to try to move him because I didn't know where he was hurt. Plus, I couldn't anyway with my injuries. I was becoming very weak very quickly. He moved his left hand over to mine and moved his head a little. I started talking to him just to try to keep him somewhat responsive and alert.

I looked over to his right arm and saw that he was bleeding out pretty badly. With my right arm still up against my stomach, I took my left hand and applied pressure to the area that was wounded to try to stop the bleeding as much as I could. I looked around, but I couldn't find anything close to me and him that I could use to put around the wound. There wasn't anything left. I just kept talking to him. I told him how much we all loved him, that we needed him, and that he couldn't leave us now. I said whatever I could think of to keep him awake.

My boys were still going around person to person helping everyone. They were not even aware of my injuries because I had always taught them that I could take care of myself and told them just to help others. There were so many injuries that night—anything from scratches and bruises to deep cuts, fractures, concussions, head injuries, back injuries, major blood loss, and internal injuries as well as external injuries. It was just unbelievable. God was most definitely with us. We were all alive, and that was all that we cared about at the time.

For some reason, something told me to turn around and look over my shoulder. So I did. I saw headlights coming off the mountain from the opposite side of us. I said out loud, "Thank You, Jesus." My son ran over to the 4Runner and started flashing the headlights. It was Tony and Daniel, our neighbors across the road from where we were at.

Tony had been my previous pastor at Bethany Baptist Church in the valley before he relocated to another church. We all knew one another as the community fairly small.

I turned back around, looked at my neighbor, and said, "Hold on for me." He nodded his head to tell me okay. With all the strength that I had left, I jumped up waving my left arm and screaming at the top of my voice as loudly as I possibly could, "Help us! Help us! Over here! Help us!" I fell down to my knees as I was so dizzy. I just knew I was fixing to pass out.

I turned back around and put pressure back on my neighbor's arm. I told him in a squeaky voice, "Hold on for me. You gotta stay with me. You can't leave me. You know I love you, my dear friend. You're like a grandfather to me. I have help on the way." Whatever it took to keep him somewhat alert. For a moment, I had forgotten about my injuries. I just would not move my right arm much, and I would not dare look at it. The back of my legs and lower back started pounding with pain. I knew the soreness was fixing to move in. But also I wasn't aware of the extent of my injuries and no one else was either.

When Tony, Daniel, and Gloria got down the mountain to us, they started going person to person as well, seeing how bad injuries were and what they could do to help. Tony told Daniel to go get blankets and whatever he could find to cover people up with. He told him to get whoever else he could, just to hurry. Tony looked at me and told me just to keep doing what I was doing, which was talking to my neighbor to keep him responsive.

I vaguely remember more people started showing up on four-wheelers trying to assist and do what they could to help. Praise Jesus! We had neighbors who walked over trees and whatever else to get to us. I don't remember who it was, but some people came over to where I was by my neighbor. I told them that they were going to have to stay with him, that I couldn't do it anymore. I had to get somewhere and lie down or something because I was beginning to get sick at my stomach and was hurting so badly. I became more and more lightheaded. I was freezing to death, and the shaking was uncontrollable.

I don't know how, but I got back over to where my daughter was sitting. The pain hit me, and I screamed. Neither boy thought or knew that I was injured badly. They were so busy helping others, but at the same time, I was trying not to show my pain to anyone. But I had this pain that ran from my neck all the way down through my groin area to my feet. Then I tried to move my arm. So it was the combination of trying to sit down and the pain that decided to hit me, and I couldn't deal with it anymore because I had been running off of adrenaline the whole time and I just didn't have any more strength.

I remember it started lightning again. I overheard someone say that the weather report just stated that Shoal Creek Valley was underneath another warning. About that time, someone brought over plastic to cover us up to try to keep us warm. Before they could get it to us, it started pouring down raining again. We were all getting drenched. All we could do was patiently sit there and wait. We were all shaking so badly and in so much pain. We were getting very weak and tired.

Finally, someone was able to get a big piece of plastic over to us. Oh! I'm sure you are all wondering about the people who were living with us. They were fine. They had a few scratches, but they were doing a lot better than the rest of us. I don't know how they kept from receiving so many injuries. But the good Lord took care of them. I was very glad that no one was killed.

As they started loading people up in the back of Daniel's truck, I remember a friend of mine coming over to check on me and Ro'chele. I remember looking up at her, shaking so badly and saying, "I can't go through it twice. Get us out of here, please. We won't make it if we go through another storm."

She calmly said, "Y'all are next. They are getting the children up in the truck and taking them to Tony and Gloria's house, and they'll be back for as many people as they can get moved."

That gave me hope. I just cowered back down as much as I could under the plastic. I sat as close as I could to my daughter to try to keep her warm. I didn't care about myself, just my baby.

Tony and Gloria used their home as a triage center and shelter for people. They knew that it would be awhile before any medical help could get to us. We started having storm after storm again. We were all so traumatized, the last thing that we needed was any more storms. *Why wouldn't they just leave us alone and go in another direction?* I kept thinking to myself. *Please God, shift the storms in another direction. We can't survive any more storms.* The wind started howling viciously again. I remember that I had started getting so cold. I must have been going into shock from all of the blood loss. I don't know, but I was shaking so badly.

You could see the truck coming back down off the mountain to load more people. They were getting all the children first. They kept that truck just constantly moving, helping people. The good Lord definitely sent us people who cared and loved us dearly to help us. They went by instinct and just started doing whatever it took to help people. I hope they know how much all of us love them.

As the wind picked back up again, I could smell gas coming from somewhere. About that time, Tony yelled out to everyone. "No one light a cigarette! We got a gas leak over here from the propane tank!"

Wow! I thought to myself. *You mean of all things, the propane tank survived?* I couldn't believe it because everything else had disappeared. There was nothing to be found. It was just absolutely gone. Vanished.

I began shaking again really badly. I was so cold. I had lost a lot of blood. More storms started approaching, and now, we had a gas leak. It seemed like the odds were working against us badly. I quietly said to myself, "Please, God, do something. Help us." I don't recall who it was because my vision was becoming a blur, but about that time, a few people came over to where we were and asked Ro'chele where she was hurt and if she could walk. Someone picked her up and started carrying her to the truck.

I watched as they slowly moved her and took her to the truck. Then I recall someone turning around to tell me, "Don't worry; I'll take good care of her." Before I go any further, let me explain to you my relationship with my children again. I have been divorced for twelve years, and I stayed that way for a reason. I raised my children in an environment of family closeness. My children were not going through life in confusion of this relationship, that relationship, or jealousy. That isn't who I am. I set the best example that I could by staying single for a reason.

My house stayed packed with kids all the time. My children invited their friends over. They all made themselves at home, and they all knew where the snacks were kept. They all called me their other mom. I loved it. It was joy to my heart. But that's how close I am to my children. They could and would always come to me for anything. I am truly blessed.

When I heard that statement "Don't worry; I will take care of her," oh no—that wasn't going to work for me. I didn't care how badly I was hurting. My child was hurt, and I was going to be with her. I didn't care how I was going to do it. I just knew that some way, I was getting up no matter what to be with her. As all mothers would say about their children, no one could take care of her like I could. I appreciated the offer at the time, but oh no, that wasn't gonna happen. No. No. No.

I started getting up. I rolled over to my left side, crying the whole time because my whole body was in so much excruciating pain. I was whispering, "Someone, help me get up." Then I repeated myself but this time, the whisper was a little louder. "Someone, help me! Please help me get up! I have to get to that truck!" Someone finally got over to me to help me get up on my feet and slowly got me to the truck.

I had been functioning off of adrenaline, and there was no more adrenaline. I had lost so much blood. I was shaking so badly from being so cold. It was a cold that I had never felt before. It wasn't like a cold feeling on a winter's day when you go outside. It was a coldness running through my veins. It is very hard to explain. It burned, that was how cold it felt in my veins. A couple of friends came over to me to help me. One of those friends happened to be my ex-husband.

As they were helping me up, one took one side of me as the other was on the opposite side holding on to me. I was slowly staggering, step-by-step. They both kept telling me to take my time, to walk slowly, that they had me and they weren't going to let me fall. I was so weak that I thought my legs were just at any time going to come out from under me and I was going to collapse.

I looked around to glance at the ones we were with. Tony and others had gotten plastic over everyone to keep them as dry and warm as possible. All I could do was start praying. "Please, Lord, help them. Don't let anyone die. They are all good people." I carefully got into the back of the truck. We were all in such desperation for medical assistance. Everyone was so tired, helpless, and we were becoming lifeless. We all just wanted to sleep.

The truck started moving slowly, transporting all of us toward the house. We had to go over trees that had fallen down everywhere. I don't know how they managed to get off that mountain to begin with. The house was on a pretty steep hill as well. But with care, Daniel slowly went over trees and carefully drove up the hill to get us to safety and out of the rain.

When we got about midway up the hill, I recall asking Gloria, who rode in the back with us, if we were going to make it. I meant, the more it rained, the harder it was making it for them to get up the steep hill. She calmly told us all that it was going to be all right and just to hold on because we were almost there. She kept all of our hopes up with comforting words, telling us, "We are going to take care of you all," and "It's going to be all right."

They started carefully unloading all of us to get us into the house and out of the weather. I happened to look down at my feet to discover that I only had one shoe on. I'd had the other one ripped off by the tornado. I was surprised I managed to keep the one that I had. It was crazy how our shirts were ripped and torn, and then here I was with one shoe. I still have it. I've kept it to this day. I figured it to be my lucky shoe.

Daniel came to the back of the truck to help me get out. I firmly told him not to touch my arm. He carefully helped me preventing any further injury and making sure that I didn't fall. I am very proud of him. He did a great job that night staying calm and doing what he had to do to help. He didn't think twice and by no means showed any nervousness.

Once I got in the house, I started looking around. There were people everywhere. The little children were lying down with blankets all over them trying to get them warmed back up. We were all muddy, wet, and bloody and had tree twigs matted up in our hair. But they didn't care. They were there to help, and they were doing everything they could. The house was a pretty big one, and, of course, we had no power so we all were doing the best we could with flashlights and whatever else we could find to use for light.

I got sat down on the couch beside my daughter. Daniel went back to help the others across the road again and to see if there was anyone else he could move up to the house with the rest of us. I remember seeing Denise, Gloria's daughter, running up the stairs to get more blankets. She came running back down and started covering the rest of us up with blankets. She saw how wet everyone was so she ran back upstairs trying to find whatever clothes she could for everybody. When she came back down the stairs this time, she had an armful and she just dropped them on the floor and started going through them. Gloria and Denise put dry clothes on everyone they could.

I remember just sitting on the couch shaking so badly. I was freezing to death. It was hard for me to keep my eyes open. I was also blocking out sound. I couldn't hear a lot of things that were being said. I was so weak. I remember opening my eyes and looking around at all the children and praising God that we were all alive. I remember looking out the living room window and seeing that the lightning was getting stronger again. I started shaking again. I was so cold, weak, and nervous.

I looked over at my daughter as Denise was getting some dry clothes on her. Ro'chele's shirt was pretty ripped up anyway. Denise gently removed her clothes and asked her how she was doing. They had to cut Ro'chele's clothes off of her to get some dry ones on her. But whatever it took, they were taking care of everyone. I remember telling her to hang in there that help was on the way and that it wouldn't be much longer. No one actually knew how long it was going to take for paramedics to get in there for all of us. But we had to stay positive and give hope to one another.

Denise wanted to try to get some dry clothes on me. I remember telling her that I was all right just to take care of everyone else. I had started shaking even more. I was just so cold. I knew I was fixing to go into shock. For some reason, I started thinking about one of the CPR classes that I had taken at work. I guess the reason I started remembering a few things about the class was because we were sitting on a leather couch. I remember being taught how to pressure point a wound. I knew if I could get my right arm positioned just right on that leather couch that I could possibly get the blood to stick to the couch and make a temporary seal on the wounds to slow the bleeding down.

Denise got dry clothes on everyone that she could and came back to me once again. She asked me one more time if she could put dry clothes on me. I whispered to her that if she could just put a lot of blankets on me because I was so cold, I thought I would be fine. She looked at me and calmly said, "Okay. I will be right back." Gloria told Denise just to start pulling blankets off the beds. Wherever she could find blankets, she was just to grab them and bring them down.

I slowly started moving my left arm without anyone noticing me and put it under my right arm. I carefully, gently, and very slowly started moving my right arm back toward the leather couch, grinding my teeth the whole time because it hurt so badly. I had lost so much blood, and that was why I was so cold. I was going into shock, and it was beginning to be extremely hard for me to stay awake. I knew I had to stay awake for my daughter though. I kept telling myself that if I could get my arm somehow, someway on that couch, I could get the bleeding to slow down some and possibly get it to clot.

That was why I was replaying CPR classes in my head. I was remembering about wounds and bleeding. I broke out into a sweat and began shaking even more because of the pain I was in trying to move my arm. I had no choice. I had to move my arm and attempt to get some of the bleeding to stop. None of us knew how long it was going to take for medical help to get to us.

I had just gotten my arm moved when Denise came back down the stairs with some more blankets for me. She had put six or seven blankets on me before I finally told her that I was getting warm. I said, "Denise, thank you."

In reply, she said, "You're welcome." She asked me if she could do anything else for me. I asked her if I gave her my daddy's cell phone number, if she could try to call him for me, and she said, "Sure."

I gave her his number, but she couldn't get out on her cell phone. The towers had been damaged as well. So we really had no way of communicating with anyone. Denise said to me, "I'm sorry; I can't get out."

I told her, "Thank you for trying." I must have fallen asleep because hours had passed before I remember waking up to the sound of many voices.

I opened my eyes and saw both of my boys. Derrell and Chase were standing in the kitchen doorway soaking wet and exhausted looking. I saw Chase with a cell phone in his hand, and I told him to call my daddy, their pawpaw, and tell him that we were okay. He said, "Yes, Momma." I heard him tell Daddy, "Hey, Pawpaw, it's Chase. Momma just wanted you to know that we were okay." I don't recall any more of their conversation.

I did not want my daddy to know any more because deep down inside, I had this gut feeling that Daddy and his boys from Pell City Street Department were on their way with equipment to clear the roads of trees and debris so the ambulances could get in to everybody. I just had this father-daughter intuition. I just knew they were on their way up with all of their big equipment, and I didn't need my daddy worrying about anything at the time.

I was so right. He and his boys had started clearing the roads. I had this sigh of relief that daddy didn't have to worry about us and that at least he knew we were alive. He could do his job a lot easier. That was why I chose to have Chase not tell him anything else. We needed ambulances and quick.

I must have fallen back to sleep because I remember waking to a lot of commotion. First responders were going around to everyone and writing down names, addresses, phone numbers, and what was wrong with them. When he got to me, I gave him the basic need-to-know information and told him that nothing was wrong with me and to take care of my daughter.

He didn't question me; he just moved on to the next person. I am sure in the back of his head he was wondering and knew that I wasn't being honest with him. But there were so many of us, he just had to keep moving to the next person so we all could be accounted for. I was so tired and weak that I ended up closing my eyes once again. I just couldn't fight it anymore. I don't know how long I was asleep this time.

I was awakened by this loud hysterical commotion from some girl. A mother of one of the kids had gotten through the trees somehow and was trying to move her son before the paramedics could check him out, and they were arguing. It made no sense whatsoever. She should have had a little common sense to let them do their job, as they were helping everybody.

Six hours later, they had gotten the roads cleared enough to start getting the ambulances in for all of us. Denise told me that her husband had told her that they had about thirty ambulances lined up from everywhere just waiting to get through to us so they could start transporting everyone to hospitals. They started with the children and getting them transported to Children's Hospital in Birmingham, Alabama.

I must have fallen asleep again because the next thing I knew, I was being awakened by a paramedic asking me if I could hear him. He wanted to know my name and where I was hurt. I calmly and in a quiet voice told him that nothing was wrong with me. He was a true paramedic, and he knew what he was doing because he simply replied, "You're lying to me."

He slowly and carefully started removing blankets off of me, layer by layer. I kept firmly exclaiming that I was fine to take care of my daughter. In reply, he explained to me that my daughter was being taken care of and that he had to take care of me and see what was going on with me.

As he carefully removed the blankets one by one, he discovered the overwhelming injuries to my right arm. It was very obvious why I was so weak and tired. There was blood everywhere—all over my clothes, the blankets, the couch. I had multiple fractures. I had bones sticking out, and my elbow had been sliced wide open. My radius bone had shattered and had shot out the side of my arm. My wrist was completely broken and dislocated and was swollen pretty badly and just dangling. Part of my elbow had been chipped off.

I had internal injuries as well. I had a hematoma the size of a grapefruit on my pelvis, more than likely from the impact of the vanity and cabinets. My kidneys had been hit so hard by debris that they were severely bruised and bleeding. From my neck down, I was severely bruised from being hit by debris. There wasn't a single spot on my back that was not bruised—evidence of having been beaten by something. It was completely black and purple.

On the top of my left hand, I had a deep cut in the shape of a C where something had just ripped the skin and peeled it back. It was bleeding, and I had a cut on my right wrist that was bleeding. I was very lucky that it didn't cut my vein because it was right there by it. I had a gash on my left hip that ran down the back side of my left leg.

We all had mud all over us and tree twigs twisted in our hair. We all had blood coming out of our ears, more than likely from the pressure when the house exploded. We had minor cuts all over our bodies. We looked like we had been in a major cat fight. I have a permanent, what I call a NIKE mark on my upper right shoulder just as perfect as it can be. I thought that was a little funny.

I would not let the paramedics move me or touch me until I had seen my daughter being put onto a stretcher. I was not going without her, and I stood firm with them on that decision. I had lived a life and wanted to make sure she was not going to get left behind. They had run out of some of the medical supplies that they needed for some of us, so they ended up using what they could find or, as I say, improvising, but it didn't matter; it still worked just as well.

They had to duct tape my daughter's head to the stretcher so her neck wouldn't move. They had to be very careful and take every precaution necessary in case of neck injuries. The next argument was that before they started moving me, I wanted us in the same ambulance. I wanted us at the same hospital getting the same help. We were not going to be in different locations spread out everywhere. I wasn't as concerned about my boys because they were old enough and mature enough to take care of themselves and make sure that we were taken care of. They agreed that they could transport us together.

They started getting me situated so they could move me onto a stretcher. As they tried to move my legs, I started screaming because of the pain. We had been waiting for six hours, and my body was so stiff when I sat up because every muscle in my body was in knots. They were fixing to start ripping the couch apart to get to me somehow to be able to move me, and about that time, Tony told them to hold up, that the couch would pull apart. One of the guys made the comment that that was the way they had done it in Springville. Tony told him that he wasn't in Springville. He was in Ashville. That was pretty hilarious. But there was no sense in them trying to mess up a brand-new couch that had recliners in it. I had to agree that was a little uncalled for.

They started again trying very carefully to get me onto a stretcher. They had put a neck brace on me and started the move. I was screaming so loudly because I was in so much pain that Tony had to leave the room. He later he told me that he just knew that my back was broken and it was just killing him inside seeing so many people hurt.

After they had gotten me on the stretcher, taped down and secured, I remember this woman coming over to me. I recognized the voice, but my vision was becoming so blurry that I couldn't make a face out with the voice. She leaned down to me and called out my name. She said, "Stacy, Ro'chele is going to be fine. She is going to be well taken care of."

I must have finally started giving up because I was so weak and tired. I must have gone unconscious for a brief period, because I don't remember being moved from the house to the ambulance. Denise later told me that as they were carrying me down the steps, every time they stepped down to another step, I would scream. I had no idea at the time that they had to load my daughter into the back of the truck and take her down to the ambulance because they had gotten an ambulance stuck in the yard and they couldn't get up through there.

I was later told that they actually carried me on the stretcher by foot down the mountain all the way to the ambulance. They couldn't take a chance of jarring me around in the back of the truck since no one knew the extent of my injuries. Not knowing if my back was broken or if there was a neck injury, they just absolutely were not going to take a chance. I was very grateful to know that they cared that much.

I vaguely remember hearing my ex-husband at the back of the ambulance once they got us both loaded up, giving them directions back to the interstate where they could get us to UAB Hospital in Birmingham, Alabama, because they were the only major trauma hospital and we both needed to be there. It was very hard for anyone that night to find the way into the valley. The community had been wiped out, and with all the damage, no one knew where they were.

Our ambulance and paramedics were from Chilton County, Alabama. Chilton County is way south of us. They are below Shelby County and beside Perry County and Coosa County. The state of Alabama had so much devastation from the tornado outbreak and there were so many communities destroyed and people injured and killed that day, they were having to use paramedics from everywhere all over the state to get help to people. They were sending whoever was available out. It did not matter how far they had to travel; they sent them on their way. I am very blessed for the Chilton County paramedics, because otherwise, there isn't much telling how long it would have taken for us to get an ambulance.

The paramedic who was in the back of the ambulance with us started an IV on my daughter. He ended up putting two IV's in because she was so dehydrated. I remember hearing him telling us both to hang in there and to talk to one another to stay awake. I couldn't open my eyes much less get the breath to speak. I was so weak and tired. All I wanted to do was just go to sleep. With what little bit of strength I had left, I began talking to Ro'chele, asking her if she was all right and telling her that we would be there soon and that I loved her. She definitely did not need to go to sleep with the head injuries that she had.

The paramedic started trying to get an IV in me. I felt so sorry for him because he tried and tried but he was not successful. I had needle holes all over my arm, but my veins were not cooperating at all. He happened to look over at my arm and see the bones hanging out and blood everywhere. He was getting upset and anxious that he couldn't get an IV to start. I remember hearing the driver telling him to keep trying that he might end up having to put it in my neck and he was going to have to do whatever he had to do.

Our drivers had gotten lost trying to get to the interstate, which was understandable because, like I said earlier, it was hard for anyone to have sense of direction or know where he or she was because of all of the damage and trees down. It was just about impossible to know where you were, even if you knew the area blindfolded. We ended up in Ragland, Alabama. I remember hearing the driver ask someone out the window if he could get him directed to the interstate. My daughter later told me that she actually helped them through to Pell City, Alabama, and onto the interstate.

We ended up pulling over on the side of the interstate because the paramedic in the back with us was getting sick to his stomach. They pulled over and switched drivers. I could hear the other paramedic asking him if he was okay, and he said, "Yes," that he would do better driving. We were soon back on the interstate. Once they got going, it didn't seem like it took them any time to get us there.

Once we got to the hospital, I heard the paramedics telling Ro'chele that they would be right back for her that they had to get me out first. I must have blacked out again because I don't even remember them rushing me through the doors into the hospital, taking me off the stretcher, and placing me onto the bed in the emergency room. I don't even remember the nurses coming in to take my vital signs or starting an IV on me.

I don't know how much time had passed. I didn't even know what time it was or anything else. I had been awakened by a nurse and a doctor who firmly called out my name. The nurse told me that they had to have a urine sample to start running some tests and start getting x-rays, a CT scan, and an MRI. I kept telling that male nurse that I had to go, but I couldn't. He firmly told me that I was either going to have to do it on my own or they were going to have to put a catheter in. I continued to tell him that I had to go but couldn't.

They finally discovered that my kidneys and bladder had taken such a bad blow they were bleeding. They catheterized me, and blood was going everywhere. I was at the point where I was just so tired again, I just wanted to sleep. I didn't care what they did to me as long as they let me sleep.

I don't know how long I was asleep because when I woke up, I was in the x-ray room. The technician had woken me up trying to move my arm to take x-rays. I was screaming bloody murder, and I told him that if he touched my arm again that I was coming up off that table and whooping his butt. I don't believe the word *butt* came out of my mouth though. He replied, "I guess I need to go get the doctor." I told him that he better bring more than the doctor back with him—more like the army back with him—because if he touched my arm one more time, I was going to hurt him.

It's kind of funny now, but they ended up sedating me very well because they were able to do x-rays, a CT scan, and an MRI and I didn't hurt anyone. But a little common sense would have told that technician that if you got bones hanging out, someone might be in just a little pain and not to be trying to straighten something that was dangling. I mean really? But anyway, they made it through it, and so did I. They must have started morphine because I don't remember anything else.

The morphine must have started wearing off after they got me back from all the tests because I opened my eyes. My ex-husband had come in there to check on me. He asked me if there was someone he could call for me, and I told him to call my daddy. Daddy's phone number was the only one that I could remember. I told him, "Just call my daddy please." I gave him his phone number.

I found out later that Daddy was devastated because he had been under the impression that all of us were all right. My ex-husband reminded him of why I had Chase tell him what I did because we had to get the roads cleared. He told him that he understood that but I was his only baby. He told Daddy that he needed to get down there pretty fast because he thought they were fixing to get me ready for surgery and he wasn't sure what all was wrong with me; he was with Ro'chele down the hall in the same hospital. Daddy told him that he was on his way.

Ro'chele's boyfriend / high-school sweetheart William, had gotten his mother to take him to the hospital so he could be with her and check on her. I am so glad that he was able to be there for her because I can only imagine how scared she must have been. I knew she was exhausted as well from trying to fight the pain and stay awake as long as she could. He came in to check on me several times. I didn't mean to worry him or anything, but I told him just to take care of Ro'chele for me and that I knew he would stay by her side.

The next thing I knew, I was being awakened going down the hallway to surgery by my orthopedic surgeon, nose to nose, asking me if he had my permission to operate. I recall nodding my head yes and replying, "I am Rh O negative."

He said, "It's going to be all right. We have you taken care of." Because of me having a rare blood type, I had always told people that I was a giver not a receiver. Anyone could take my blood type because I was compatible with anyone, but I couldn't receive from anyone unless they were O negative. They could always give me the Rhogam shots, but I couldn't receive from just anyone. My half- sister wasn't even O negative.

Then I absolutely remember nothing else. They had given me everything I needed for surgery, and I was out cold. I had no idea what they were operating on, what all was wrong with me, or if my daughter and sons were okay. I did know that I had bones out of my arm, but I had no idea what all they were going to have to do to save my arm. I do know that every day of my life, I am very thankful for my surgeon. He took such good care of me.

I was so weak and tired and had lost so much blood that I didn't know anything for about three days. There were hit-and-miss things that I remembered after surgery but not a lot. For the biggest portion, I was told about it. I don't remember my dad being there or even when he got there. I didn't know anything about my children and if they were all right or what their injuries were. I just had no clue about anything.

I felt terrible because, like I said before, I couldn't remember anyone's phone number but my dad's. I am going to tell you how my mother and sister found us. They knew that the tornado had come through Shoal Creek Valley because of the news, but they also knew that I had always told my family not to ever worry about us, that I would get myself and the kids out of the way before it ever hit.

When they couldn't get through the phone lines or my cell phone, they began to worry a little bit. They waited it out through the night thinking that I would eventually call them and that the reason I hadn't called was probably because of the phone lines being down and the cell phone towers being so busy with everyone trying to call out.

Well, they both had waited as long as they were going to wait.

My mother had called my sister and asked her which one of them was going to go hunt for us or if she wanted to go with her. My sister told her to go on since she was the closest and just in case my sister needed to start searching the hospitals in Birmingham, Alabama.

It took Mother a little while to get up through the valley, and then she had to wait in line because all of the county deputies had their cars at different ins and outs of the valley trying to keep sightseers and looters out. They were still trying to do head counts for everyone and for each address. They had people help them mark the ones that they knew were at the hospitals and which ones weren't. It had to be difficult for all of them. I know we are a small community, but besides just the small damage, a total of three hundred homes were completely wiped off the map. Nowhere to be found. Mine was one of them.

Mother finally got onto Shoal Creek Road, and she explained to the deputy who she was and that she was trying to find us. He let her on through after she gave him our address. Once she got down to the property, she was in complete shock because there was no house, only a concrete foundation. None of us were around, and she began to panic.

Daniel happened to be down at his sister Denise's house. She lived on the other side of me. Daniel told her where we were, and she jumped in the car headed to UAB. She called my sister and told her so she headed that way also. It took them a little while once they got to UAB; they still had people in the hallways getting treatment because there were no rooms available to move them into. UAB is the only major trauma hospital in the state of Alabama. We had over fifty tornadoes that day. So you can imagine how many people were there. They were transferring people from all over the state to UAB. They even had Red Cross buses outside the hospital lined up getting people to donate blood.

The faculty didn't mean to be so ugly to family members trying to find their loved ones, but the hospital was at full capacity. They had to call in over 144 surgeons that night. That is not even including the nurses and other doctors. The staff was very stressed, had limited space and hundreds upon hundreds of patients to help, and didn't even really know where anyone was. But they finally found me.

I don't know if I was still in surgery, out of surgery, or what when they found me. I was in a different world by then. I don't even remember my boys finding me. I didn't even know that my dad was there. I remember giving my ex-husband his number and permission to my surgeon to do my surgery, and then everything else I have no intellectual remembrance of.

I was so weak and tired and had lost so much blood that I didn't know anything for three days. There were hit-and-miss things that I remember after surgery but not a lot. I was told about a lot of things because I was out cold. I do remember waking up one time telling my mother to get that neck brace off of me or I was going to take it off. I must have gotten out of hand with it, because a nurse had come into the room and I remember hearing her tell my mother that she would have to check with the doctor and make sure my CT scans and MRI results were cleared before they could remove the brace.

I must have fallen back to sleep for a little while because the next thing I recall was when the nurse came back into my room and was telling me that she was going to remove the brace for me because the doctor said that it was okay. When she did, it was like the best feeling of relief that I'd ever had. I could finally breathe, but my neck was so stiff. My nurse started telling me that if I had any pain that I had a morphine pump. She placed this gadget in my hand and told me that I had a red button on the end of it and all I had to do was press it and it would release the medication to me.

I must have pushed the button quite often because my life was a blur for a couple of days. Like I said earlier, I don't remember a lot about the hospital stay. My mother, sister, and aunt took turns staying with me while I was in the hospital. I woke up one time in the middle of the night and started looking around trying to figure out where I was.

When I halfway started coming around a little more, I was extremely anxious after I looked over and saw my right arm with this huge bandage; actually, it was what they called a half-soft and half-hard cast. It was from the tips of my fingers all the way up above my elbow and halfway up to my shoulder. I had all of these pillows under me stabilizing my arm to get some of the swelling down.

My left hand was bandaged so that it looked like I had a boxing glove on. As I was trying to figure it all out, a nurse came in and said, "Ms. Landry, I am here to give you your blood thinner shot. It has to go in your stomach, but you won't feel a thing."

I looked at my stomach and saw all these pin-needle-sized holes. So I figured they had been giving them to me for a while. I looked at her with my blurred vision and said, "Okay."

Then there was this time that I had started hurting pretty badly. My nephew was there, and he calmly looked over at me and said, "Aunt Stacy, do you want me to push the red button for you?"

I said, "Yes, please," and then I was out again. The only thing I can say is morphine is a wonder drug because when I start hurting really badly I can be a handful.

Mother had woken me up one day because I had a special visitor. Brian, my supervisor, and my best friend, Max, had found me and come to check on me. I remember asking Brian where Max was, and he said, "He is outside the door." Brian told me that Max couldn't handle seeing me hurt at the time, but they had to find me and check on me.

I was in a state of shock when Brian told me that. I started wondering if something was wrong with my face. Was part of my hair missing? I mean, what was it? Why wouldn't he come in and see that I was alive? I was just really confused about the situation. Mother must have seen the confusion on my face because she quickly changed the subject. She asked me if I felt like sitting up so she could show Brian my back and neck.

Then I started thinking again. "What is wrong with my back and neck?" I asked Mother. "What is it?" She replied that she wanted to show Brian how badly I had been beaten by debris. She had taken pictures at some point on her phone of my back and neck. I don't even remember her doing that at all.

With everyone's help, she carefully leaned me forward and then the next thing I heard was, "Oh my goodness!" I was tired after I had leaned up. It took a lot out of me just to move that little bit. My whole body was in pain. I don't even remember what they were saying after she had showed him because I was just in that much pain. It was one of those moments where you know someone is saying something, but you just can't hear them talking; it's a bunch of chatter to you. Mother gave me my pain medication, and things went to a blur again.

When I woke up this last time, I was full of energy. I must have slept awhile. I woke up as if nothing had happened, and I was ready to get up out of the bed and get to moving. I was hungry too. I didn't know how many days it had been since I had eaten last. I was craving a bacon cheddar roast beef sandwich from Arby's. My brother-in-law and nephew went and got me Arby's. I was eating the sandwich like it was going out of style, like I was never going to have another one like it again. I was starving. It was the best sandwich that I had ever eaten.

When I got through eating, I started looking around to see all these different lines hooked up to me. I was trying to figure out what this line went to, where that line went to, what they all did, and why I had so many. Mother explained to me that I had a line to monitor my heart and I had one for my blood pressure, my pain pump, my IV, the antibiotics, and I can't remember what she said the little third bag was for, some type of other medication that I needed. Then there was the dreadful catheter line. I promise you, I was not going to try to escape with all those lines and machines. I had stuff going on everywhere. I was questioning myself, *Is this all really necessary?*

Mother asked me if I wanted to see with a mirror. At first, I thought to myself that I didn't know if I wanted to or not. I didn't want any more surprises. Then I decided to look. I had a few places on my face, a couple of scratches here and there, but nothing like I really was expecting. The funniest thing was seeing my hair. It was all bushy and matted. My mother kind of snickered for a moment. She said, "Your sister has been working on your hair for three days now. She has been pulling grass, dirt, and twigs out. She tried to brush it and dry shampoo it, but it just didn't work out too well." I just smiled and giggled a little because I was still in a lot of pain and I knew if I laughed like I really wanted to, I would be in trouble and would have to have more morphine. I really wanted to stay awake for a little while.

I stayed awake a lot longer this time, and I even felt like trying to get a shower. My nurse was coming in and out checking on me, taking my vital signs, and bringing me different medications that I needed. By looking at all of my lines, you wouldn't have thought that I needed anything else, but I had to take other medications besides what they were already giving me. I felt well enough that I asked Mother and my sister about taking a bath or shower. They went and talked with the nurse about it, and she told them that she would have to take a look at some of my tests results and blood work and ask the doctor if I could take a bath yet or not. That didn't make any sense to me. I figured they would want me to stay as clean as possible especially with open and closed wounds, but, hey, I was not a doctor either.

It wasn't too long before the nurse came back into my room and said that the doctor had said that as long as I felt up to it and wasn't dizzy or anything, that I could try it. Then she said, "I'll be right back where we can take the catheter out."

I thought to myself, *Oh boy. Where is the pain medication at?* While she was removing everything including the heart monitor lines, my sister went on into the bathroom and started fixing the shower for me. She had gotten one of those chairs to sit on while you were taking a shower because I really didn't need to try to stand up for very long just yet. It was a good thing she did that because I probably would have fallen out on them from being so lightheaded and dizzy.

My sister had the shower running for me getting the water nice and warm. Then she and my mom slowly, step-by-baby-step, got me to the bathroom. It took all the strength that I had just to get to the shower, but I was very determined to smell just a little better. I knew I would feel a lot better once I got cleaned up a little.

All I had on was that stupid hospital gown, so it wasn't hard for them to undress me and get it over my arms with all the bandages, my cast, and my IV's that I still had in. I just sat there once I got into the shower and let the water run over my head. I didn't want to move because it felt so good. While I had my head down, allowing the water to run over the back of my head and neck, I looked down at the drain, and I saw all this dirt and Lord knows what else coming off of me and out of my hair.

Everybody kept checking in on me because I was in there for so long, but it just felt so good to have a shower. I absolutely did not want to get out. Every time they would come in, I would tell them that I was fine that this was the best shower that I had had in a while. As I was bathing, I decided to get a little brave and attempt to shave my legs with my left arm because I could move it and I knew they would have to put a dry bandage on after I got through anyway.

My body was numb from all of the medications that I had to have. I had actually cut myself somewhere, and blood was running down the drain badly. I figured the bleeding would eventually stop once I got out of the shower. Boy was I mistaken. I had started a huge commotion with everyone because blood was still going everywhere. And it was all because of a small cut from shaving my legs. Needless to say, the blood thinner shots were doing exactly what they were supposed to do.

I called Mother and my sister to come help me out, and I was standing there with blood all over the floor. The nurse just happened to walk into the room at the same time. It was pretty funny because the nurse hysterically said, "Oh my gosh, there is blood everywhere!" Then she said, "Wait a minute. I'm a nurse. I can handle this." I explained to her what had happened. They got the bleeding to stop and got me back in bed. I was about ready for a nap after all of that excitement. I decided to sit up in bed for a while. Mother and my sister raised my bed up a little for me and fixed all of my pillows under my arm once again. I felt human again after my shower.

I don't remember what day it was or how long I had been in the hospital, but I do remember when the doctor came in and checked on me and explained what they had had to do to me. I had pins in my wrist because it had been dislocated. They had to smooth down what was left of my elbow, and I had stitches there. I had multiple fractures to my right radius bone, and they had to put a plate and screws there to hold my bones together. They had to put staples there instead of stitches.

The doctor started explaining to us that so many people were severely hurt and had been transported to UAB Hospital that they were actually having to treat and take care of patients in the hallways because they had no open rooms. The emergency room, surgery rooms, and all floors were at full capacity. He continued to explain to us the care of all my wounds and what had to be done, and he talked about all my medications that I had to take, what he was prescribing, and when I needed to return to the doctor's office.

He was going to go ahead and release me, but we had to take extreme precautions and take care of all of my wounds as he told us or I could end up with serious infections. They were having to release as many as they could with instructions for care at home because they needed more rooms to treat other patients who were coming out of surgeries. In other words, they were shipping in and shipping out as quickly as possible to get as many people transported and treated because these other hospitals didn't have the technology or doctors that UAB did. This was completely understandable because there were hundreds upon hundreds of people who had been severely injured. It didn't bother me one bit. I was ready to get out of there.

My sister really wanted me to come stay at her house with them because they lived in Birmingham and that way if something happened, they could get me back to the hospital a lot quicker than if I was at Mother's house or Daddy's house, but I insisted on going with Mother because all I wanted to do was go check on my kids and my house.

No one dared to tell me anything about my home or about my neighbors or for that matter the whole community while I was in the hospital. Honestly, I would not have comprehended anything that they had tried to tell me anyway because I was so heavily sedated. My sister knew and understood why I wanted to go home. It had nothing to do with who I was with or who could take care of me; as far as I was concerned, I could take care of myself because I was just that independent.

I just needed to be closer to my children and closer to where I could get someone to take me to see my home. We were all so displaced it was unbelievable. I had no idea where my boys were staying. I didn't even know who my daughter was with, and it was killing me. I had no idea what my valley looked like either. I was clueless and completely helpless.

I vaguely remember being wheeled out of the hospital. I don't remember getting in the car or if I even told my sister how much I loved her. But I do remember when my mother stopped at Walgreens to get all my medications filled. I insisted on getting out with her, which was a huge mistake. I wanted to get a hairbrush and some makeup. I started feeling so weak and dizzy. I told her that I had to go back to the car and that I would be all right and could make it to the car on my own.

For some reason, I needed a pack of cigarettes and a lighter. I don't know where I got the money from, but somehow, I had a twenty-dollar bill. I don't even know who gave it to me. At the time, all I cared about was that I had money and wanted a pack of smokes. I told the sweet cashier what I wanted, and I thought I was fixing to pass out on her right then. I kept thinking, *Lord, let me get to the car because if I pass out in this store, they are going to be calling an ambulance, and I will be back in the hospital.*

I got checked out and slowly started toward the door. Now this part gets a little funny. I had to lean up against the outside of the building for a minute because I was so dizzy. There were people looking at me like I don't know what. I kept thinking, *Have y'all people never seen someone that just got out of the hospital?* I looked down at my feet and clothes, and then I realized why they were looking at me weirdly.

Well, of course I had no clothes except for the bloody ones that I came to the hospital in, and my nurse at the hospital had found me a pair of scrubs to wear home. No one thought about running down to a store while I was in the hospital and grabbing me a shirt and a pair of sweats because they didn't want to leave my side.

As I was leaned up against the building, yeah, I looked like crap. I mean I just survived an EF4 tornado, and with all my bandages and cast, it wasn't a pretty sight. I happened to look over where this couple was sitting in their car, and they had this surprised look about them as they were watching me staggering out the door. I was tired, weak, in pain, and of all things sick at my stomach. So I had one of those outburst moments of rudeness and yelled, "What? You never seen someone that just got out of the hospital before?"

It didn't dawn on me at the time because of me being in scrubs that they were probably thinking, *Dang, she had a heck of a night at work.* But anyway, who knows? It's hard to read people; there isn't much telling what they were thinking. I finally got on over to Mother's car and lit that cigarette that I just had to have, and boy was that a mistake! I started getting dizzier and then got sick at my stomach. I was thinking, *Lord, help me. I am going to die right here in Walgreens parking lot.*

I managed to crank up Mother's car and turned the air conditioner on full blast. I needed some air and fast. I kept thinking, *This cold air has got to help because I am sweating like crazy from getting sick.* My mouth started watering again, and all I could think was, *Here we go again. Please don't let anyone be watching because I can't control it.* I kept saying to myself, "Mother, hurry up. Come on and hurry up. It can't be taking that long. It's not like we are buying every drug in the pharmacy. I gotta get out of here, and I need to get home now. Come on, Mother! I need to lie down somewhere and preferably not back at the hospital."

Twenty minutes later, Mother finally came out of Walgreens and saw me white as a sheet. She said, "Oh, baby, I'm sorry it took so long." Then she said, "But I did get you a pair of house shoes."

I sat there a minute with this strange look on my face and thought about it a second. I looked down at my feet and started laughing. The hospital had put a pair of those socks with grippers on my feet. She asked me what was so funny. I said, "You mean the store let me go in without shoes on?"

She just laughed and said, "Well, I don't guess they were worried about your feet."

I must have fallen asleep because I don't remember anything about the car ride. Mother woke me up when we got to our destination, and we were definitely not at my house. We were at my mother's and aunt's house. Mother started getting me out of the car, and my aunt came over to help her because I had to climb up concrete steps to get on the front porch. I told them to take me over to the front porch swing because I wanted to sit there a few minutes and I wanted a cigarette. They both looked at me and said, "Okay."

I wasn't out there long. I just wanted to try to regather my thoughts, get a fresh breath of air, and hear the birds sing a minute. I was so clueless about things, and I just wanted a little bit of comfort. I mean, I was still in shock. I still couldn't believe what we had just gone through. I would have never thought in a million years that a tornado would come down our beautiful valley. We had mountains behind us and across the road. You would have thought that you were in one of the safest places that you could be in. I always called it God's country.

Mother and my aunt came and got me and brought me on inside the house. They sat me down in the recliner and had pillows to place under my arms to keep the swelling down as much as possible. They covered me up and gave me all my medications. They tried to get me to eat something. But I just didn't have much of an appetite. They turned a movie on, and I must have slept all night because when I woke up, it was morning.

My aunt and mother were making coffee, and I remembered that I had promised Max that I would call him when I got out of the hospital. I thought now that I was out of the hospital, maybe he would come see me. Before I called him, I was trying really hard to figure out what day it was. I asked Mother, and she said it was Saturday. I knew then that he didn't have an excuse not to be able to come see me because he would be working at one of the plants that was really close to where I was.

I called him and told him I was out of the hospital and where I was. We talked for a few minutes, and then he told me that he would run by and see me when he got off work. Mother had fixed me a cup of coffee. It sure was good; I didn't know how many days it had been since I'd had a good cup of coffee, and it hit the spot. It's something about that morning caffeine.

I felt like getting up and moving around a little to see if I could get all the muscles in my body to loosen up a little. My whole body felt like it was in this huge ball of a knot. I walked out onto the back porch a minute while they were cooking breakfast. They were going to try to get me to eat something, but I just didn't have an appetite.

A little time had passed, and my best friend Max drove up. I was so excited that I met him on the front porch before he had a chance to get out of his truck. I just wanted to greet him and give him this huge hug. I didn't want to let him go. He was my safe haven, someone who would just hold me and let me cry if I wanted to cry on his shoulder. I had always been able to tell him anything, and it didn't matter what it was. We would laugh together and cry together, but we never got mad at each other.

We gave each other a hug like we hadn't seen each other in years. I don't know which one of us was happier. Both of us were happy, I believe, because all of us were alive. I could see the look in his eyes and knew he was so worried about me and the kids. I showed him my back and neck and how bruised they were. I tried to reassure him that I was going to be all right.

He told me that he had tried to call my house and my cell phone the night the tornado hit. But he couldn't get through to me; the phones would just ring and ring. He said that when I didn't show up for work the next day, he started worrying even more. When I still didn't show up at 7:30 a.m. that next morning, he started pacing the floors because I always called him if I was going to be late.

Someone had brought in one of the local newspapers, and on the front page was my car. It had been twisted and mangled between trees and was up on its side. Max went hysterical and ran into Brian's office to show him the paper. Max had this gut feeling that something was wrong. He told Brian to start calling people to find me. At first, they really didn't know where to start.

Brian thought about Shane, another guy that we had all worked with at the Lincoln, Alabama, plant. Shane started calling people we all knew at Pell City, Alabama, and got my dad's cell phone number. They called Daddy, and he told them that I was at UAB and in surgery. But they found me. It's not every day that people can say that they work with a wonderful group of people like I do. They cared enough to find me. That should give anyone chills.

I told Max that I was so sorry that they had to find out that way. He told me that he had not been that scared in a very long time. I told him that when I looked up and saw the tornado coming for us I dropped my purse on the front porch, which had my cell phone in it. I told him there wasn't much telling where it ended up. He gave me a small crack of a smile, not much though. Then he hugged me, kissed my forehead about ten times, and told me that he was so happy to see me. He drank a cup of coffee with me, and then he had to leave. It brought joy to my heart to see him even though he couldn't stay long.

Max got into his truck and started to leave. He gave me a wave bye, and it took all that I had to hold back the tears. As I watched him leave, tears started running down my cheeks. I was so happy that I was able to see him, and at the same time, I was so sad that he was leaving.

I went back inside and asked Mother when she thought we could ride up to the house so I could check on things. She had this look and asked me if I thought I would be up to it. I told her that I had my medications and that I would be fine; I just needed to go check on the house and see how much damage if any had been done.

As everyone was getting ready and changing clothes, I briefly watched a little of the local news. I had not seen any of the reports because I had been so heavily sedated at the hospital. I knew that it had been bad, but I had no idea of the severity of the damage throughout the whole state of Alabama. As I was watching, they never showed any reports on Shoal Creek Valley. They were showing all the damage in places like Tuscaloosa, Pratt City, and Hackelburg.

It was just unbelievable seeing the damage in those towns. It was like nothing was left of any of them except rubble. You couldn't make out what anything was or where it used to be. I felt so bad for all of those people. They were interviewing survivors, and they were speechless. It was a very bad situation for everyone. The entire state.

Mother and my aunt got me into the car with all of my pillows and made sure I had something to drink in case I had to take any of my medications while we were gone. Still no one dared to tell me or prepare me for what I was fixing to endure. It broke their hearts so badly that they just couldn't tell me. It was probably for the best that I did see it for myself because I don't think I would have believed anyone.

We started on our commute toward Ashville, Alabama. My sister had called my mother, and she decided just to meet her and her husband at Ashville High School before we went down to the valley. They thought it was better that we all went together. My dad and my stepmom were going to meet us there as well.

When we arrived at the school, there were people everywhere outside. Cars were lined up everywhere. I still had no idea what was going on. A friend of mine greeted us at the car and gave me a big hug. She was so glad to see me. She told us to go inside the school, that they had all kinds of supplies and clothes, and to go see if there might be something that I could use. I really didn't want anything because I was expecting to go back to my home. In my mind, I was thinking I had everything that I needed. I had clothes and food in the fridge. *What more do I need?* I thought.

Finally, my sister arrived, and she and my mother were talking where I couldn't really hear them. We all loaded up and left, going toward the valley. My dad had already gotten there ahead of us, which was a good thing. Still no one told me anything. When we got to the stop sign at Shoal Creek Valley, there were county deputies everywhere and we had to give them our address and purpose of coming through the valley.

Mother gave them my address, and we started going through. They kept asking me as we went down the road if I was okay, and I would reply, "I am fine." It was shocking, seeing all the trees down everywhere. Debris was piled up on top of debris. I didn't even recognize a lot of homes because there was just that much destruction.

We got closer to my neighbor's house, where we were when the tornado hit, and I was amazed because there was nothing left. Bethany Baptist Church had damage. There was a huge dent on the side of the church where a cow had been tossed into the side of it. The church steeple was barely hanging on. All I could do was shake my head and ask why.

There was an older house that had been shoved over and off its foundation. There might have been a wall or two left in it. Just heartbreaking. We got closer to my house, and my neighbors' homes were nowhere to be found. I started looking for my house, and I was just shocked. I was getting sick at my stomach. I just couldn't believe what I was seeing.

We came on down my driveway toward the property. All I had was a concrete foundation left. My home was nowhere to be found. There was so much debris everywhere. We had trees mangled on top of one another and twisted like I never knew they could be twisted. My car was across the street on its side in between trees with the axles blown out.

My mind went completely blank. I didn't know what to feel or think. There was tin from everywhere just twisted around trees. The trees that were left looked like toothpicks because they had been stripped of their bark and limbs. There were concrete blocks from people's homes just lying everywhere. All you could do was say that you thought they belonged to your house.

You could look at the side of the mountain and see where the tornado had ridden the side of it and then when it came back down off of it. It was like it was trying to go over the mountain, but it just couldn't get over it. When it came back down off the mountain, it came straight back down on my house. That was why we couldn't find anything. It just took it and threw it everywhere. Who knows where?

This tornado was so powerful that it had driven two-by-four pieces of wood straight down into the ground. You couldn't even budge them with your hands. There was a music CD that had been thrown like a knife and was stuck inside what was left of a tree in our yard. I had never seen anything like it before, not even on television. It had even ripped the anchor bolts from the house out of the ground.

I was so heartbroken. Everything I had worked for was gone and nowhere to be found. My car, which I almost had paid off, was destroyed. All I could do was walk around in this daze, as if I was going to wake up at any moment, as if none of this had ever happened. I would just walk and walk, as I didn't know where I was or what I was going to do. I just kept walking around in hope that I would find something, just anything that once belonged to us. But there just wasn't anything.

I walked down the driveway a little bit to get away from everyone. I needed to cry, scream, do something because I was just so angry. I broke down in tears. I was completely helpless and didn't know where even to begin with any of this. I couldn't believe that this was happening to us. I just kept saying, *Why?* over and over in my head.

I walked back up to where everybody was. I had started hurting and needed my medications. I was crying so much that I couldn't stop, and my head was even killing me. I didn't care who saw me crying. I had just lost everything I ever owned, and I didn't know what to do. My sister came over to me and asked me if I was okay, and I didn't even know what to say because I was in that much shock.

This piece of tin was wrapped around and lodged into trees by the EF4 tornado that was on the side of my property.

This is the concrete foundation that my home once sat on. The EF4 tornado shattered cinderblocks and ripped wire up from everywhere. This piece of tin was from my neighbor's shop.

The EF4 tornado took this sweet gum tree in my front yard and snapped it in half.

My car ended up across the wooded area from where my house used to be, on its side. The axles under the car where completely broken in half, and the tires were hanging on by a small piece of metal. The trunk was shoved inside the backseat of the car, and the windows were either shattered or blown out.

Pictured here is "Axle," one of the two golden retrievers, our family pets, who survived the tornado and destruction. Both retrievers stayed in shock for months after the storm, and to this day, they know when a storm is coming close and seek shelter.

This wooden plaque was hanging on the wall in my utility room. It was found on the property after the storm. It sustained hardly any damage besides a few scratches.

This was and still is Bethany Baptist Church in Shoal Creek Valley. The church sustained a lot of damage but was restored months later. The church is not even a half of a mile from where my house sat.

I started trying to clear my mind and think. I told everyone that I needed to get in touch with the insurance company but I didn't have the number because it was in my purse. I had forgotten that a few years back, I had given Daddy copies of all of my insurance papers on everything from the house to accidental death policies that I had.

He looked over at me and told me that it was all right that he and my sons had called everyone who needed to be called. It was all taken care of. I said, "Okay." The kids' uncle was bringing the boys a camper to stay on at the property. My daughter was with her daddy, and I decided that I would go to my daddy's and stay a few nights. I had to figure out something and quick. My sister had already applied for assistance for me. One of Derrell and Chase's friends was bringing over a tractor so they could push some of the trees up in a pile. I didn't want them doing a whole lot until the insurance company came out.

None of us stayed long at the property. It was too depressing to sit there and look at all of the destruction. I had to get out of there. I couldn't look at it and what was left of our community, which was absolutely nothing anymore. We all decided to leave because we were going to have to come back the next day and we would probably be there all day waiting on the insurance company.

I was getting weak, so Daddy got me into the truck and we headed back to his house where I could lie back down and get some rest. I didn't have a lot to say all the way back home. Daddy knew, so he didn't even try to make conversation. He understood that I was confused and if I wanted to talk, I would.

We got back to his house, and he tried to get me to eat something, but I just wanted to lie down. I couldn't eat because I was just so sick at my stomach from seeing all the destruction. Food was the last thing on my mind.

I was very restless all night long. I would sleep a couple of hours and wake up. It was constant all through the night. I tried to get up out of Daddy's big recliner during the night, but I couldn't move. So I just lay there and hoped that I could go back to sleep. I didn't think morning would ever get there.

I eventually fell back to sleep for a while and Daddy woke me up to check on me. They had put some coffee on and were going to fix some breakfast. I just wanted a cup of coffee, but Daddy made me try to eat a little so I could start building my strength back up some. We all took showers and got ready to head up toward the property again.

The boys had the camper set up and functioning for them to stay in. Ro'chele decided that she wanted to stay with a close friend of hers for a while. There was really nothing that we could do at the property but sit there and look at the destruction. A FEMA representative called me and said they were coming up in a day or so to take an assessment of all of the damage.

Really the only reason I wanted to go up to the property was to check on the kids, spend a little time with them, and make sure that they were all right physically and mentally. We had been through a lot, and it was just way too much to take in at one time like we were all having to do. It was killing me being away from my children, but we were all displaced and scattered out everywhere. There was nothing that I could do about it at the time, but at least everyone had a place to stay.

I figured it would be better for Ro'chele to be with her close friends because it might be easier for her to talk and get what she felt out with them than with me right then. Plus, I was on so many medications, I wasn't coherent half the time anyway. I was glad that the boys had the camper because they wanted to stay on the property and protect whatever we might have had left, which was nothing. But it just made them feel better to stay there, so I didn't have a problem with that.

I visited with the kids for a while. I saw how the boys had the camper set up and made sure that they had food. I walked around the property again for a little while. I was hoping that I would come across something that belonged to us. But when the tornado landed on the house, it was so strange because it pulled up grass and dirt and shoved it everywhere. There wasn't much telling what all was buried underneath the dirt. But my hopes were crushed because I found nothing.

Ro'chele was getting tired and ready to leave. It hurt her just like the rest of us to see the property. All of their baby stuff and belongings acquired up to that day in time were gone. It had all just vanished. It was hard for anyone to see. So we all decided to call it a day. Until the insurance company came out, we really couldn't do anything anyway. We didn't want to touch anything so they could see the whole and complete destruction.

I hugged my children and tightly. I didn't want to let them go. I didn't care about the material things. All I cared about was that we were all alive. I told them how much I loved them, and as we all started getting into vehicles, I started crying again because the last thing I wanted to do was be away from my children any longer than I had to be. It was killing me inside because we were all so displaced.

We needed each other the most right then. I couldn't imagine what all was going through their minds. And I hated them seeing me all bandaged up and the way I was. I felt so helpless because I couldn't be there for them and I couldn't do anything to fix it and make it all go away. I was the one who was supposed to be taking care of them, and I couldn't.

When we got back to my daddy's, I sat out on the front porch for a while in a daze. I was trying to think, but I was just numb. Daddy came out, hugged me, and told me that it was going to be all right. He said, "The kids are fine. They are being taken care of, and you have to take care of yourself. You can't begin to start healing if you don't start eating."

I looked at him with tears, and I calmly said, "I know. But it just hurts, Daddy. It hurts seeing my children's home is gone. We have no place to call home. All we have is a piece of land. I have no car. I have nothing. I don't even have a license." All he could do was hug me.

Daddy felt the pain with me, and I know it hurt him as badly as it did me. He was as helpless as I was. Daddies always fix things, and he couldn't fix this. I saw tears in his eyes one time, but I didn't let him know that I had seen. He knew he had to stay strong for me the best that he could, and he couldn't if he showed what he felt for me. His strength helped me more than anything not to give up, because it would have been very easy for me to give up.

I finally went on inside and took a shower. After I had undressed, I decided to take a look at my injuries. My stomach was black and purple from the bruising and all the shots that I had to have. I had cuts everywhere, and a lot of them they would not put stitches in because they wanted and needed the wounds to heal from the inside out. I finally turned around and looked at my back, and I just could not believe what I was seeing. I know one thing; I will never forget the pain from the blows that I took from debris that night. I was very surprised that my back didn't receive fractures or completely break by the way it looked in the mirror.

I slowly lifted my legs over into the shower. I was so sore all over my body it hurt sometimes even to walk, but I had to in order to try to get the tensed muscles to relax a little. I took my time. I must have taken too long because my stepmom came in and checked on me. I ended up having to have her help to get dressed anyway. It was a little hard considering that one arm was in a cast and the other looked like a huge boxing glove with all of the bandages.

I attempted to eat a little bit of dinner, but my stomach just wasn't ready to handle food. I was a nervous wreck and hurting. All I wanted to do was lie down and cry myself to sleep. I knew none of it would go away, but at least I would feel a little better—or I thought I would—if I just had a good cry. My dad gave me all my medications, fixed my pillows for me, turned the television on, and gave me the remote in case I felt like watching anything to help me go to sleep. But every channel had something on about the tornado outbreaks, and I would replay the events of that night in my head.

The next morning, Daddy had to go into work for just a little while. I was sitting outside and started thinking about my license, my bank account, and my cell phone. I went inside and told my stepmom that I needed to go to town and take care of those things because there wasn't much telling where any of my bank checks were and if someone got a hold of them, they could just start writing checks everywhere and that was the last thing that I needed.

We went to the bank first and got the accounts changed, and I got another debit card ordered and a few checks printed off in case if I needed them. The next stop was the courthouse. I had no identity showing who I was, so I had to get my license again. I could have killed my stepmom though. She and a couple of her coworkers were trying to get me to smile a little, and anyway, they made me laugh all crazy like when the lady took my picture for my license. I looked like I was a drunk laughing at a good joke. It is kind of funny now, and all they were doing was trying to get my mind off of everything, but it was just so hard.

I had walked outside for a little while waiting on my stepmom. She had a couple of things she had to take care of at work before we left. It didn't bother me any. I was enjoying the peace and quiet outside. It was one of those moments when I just wanted to be by myself anyway. As I sat outside, I did receive a lot of strange looks, but no one bothered asking me any questions. I was happy about that because at the time, the last thing I wanted to do was relive that day right then.

She met me outside, and we went to our next destination, which was to see about my cell phone. They were able to turn the other one off wherever it might have landed and still give me the same phone number that I previously had. They even gave me a discount on another phone. I was really hoping that they would just give me another one without charging me anything, but they couldn't so I just took what they could do for me.

We had to go by Walgreens and pick up the other half of my prescriptions. They were only able to fill half of them because they had run out of the medications. My doctor had prescribed two of my pain medications for me to take every two to four hours, so I had a lot of pills and they had to order the rest of them.By the time we got through, my dad was on his way home from work. We had to head toward the valley to go meet some people who were going to take a look at things for some type of assistance.

On the way up to Shoal Creek Valley, I kept looking out the window at all of the tree damage even on Highway 231. It was just so hard to let it all sink in that this had happened to us. But at the same time, I knew that I was going to have to get past my emotions in order to move forward. I was hoping that we would be able to get some type of assistance.

As a victim of such a devastating natural disaster, all you want is someone to care, and there were thousands upon thousands of people who needed help. So many people were hurt mentally and physically, and it was going to take everyone to come together to help the victims become survivors.

The representative that I had was a female. I felt a little better about that because if I were to start crying on her, at least she could sympathize with me. I am not saying that men don't cry; I am just saying I felt more comfortable at the time having a female representative.

She looked around at everything and was just amazed as the rest of us were about the destruction and the size of the tornado that came through the valley. She started taking pictures of everything—the blocks that were left, the concrete foundation where the house used to sit, and even the trees. She put all of the pictures on her computer, and once she was through, we sat down under the canopy so she could start all of the paperwork.

It was a good thing that I had gone and gotten myself another license because she had to have some type of identification in order to start the paperwork—a picture showing who I was and my address. I was so glad I had thought about that earlier or I would not have been able to start the process until I did get some type of picture identity.

All that would have done was postpone the process for at least two weeks before she would have been able to get back to me. She just had so many people that she had to do paperwork for.

She was very nice to all of us. She took the time to talk to us and showed that she cared and that she was so sorry that we had to go through this type of experience. She was very glad that we all lived to be able to tell the story one day. I was very pleased with her because she was in no hurry to rush into all these questions that she had to ask; instead, she spent one-on-one time with us all.

We finally started getting into the paperwork part of filing the claim. It was question after question and explanation after explanation, but she took as much time as needed for each one to be logged in the system properly. I would say that it took us about two and a half hours to do everything, but it had to be done. She was processing it that day because it would take a couple of weeks before we would know what type of assistance we might be able to get from whichever organization.

I was relieved that at least that part was over with. Before she left to go to the next household, as we were sitting there talking about things, it was such a coincidence that this SUV pulled up in what was left of my yard. It was a lady I knew of, along with two gentlemen from the Elks Lodge. They were out visiting people and talking with them to see if there was anything that they could do to help.

My face was red from crying. I was at that breaking point, and I couldn't hold my emotions in any longer. So the tears were flowing left and right, but I couldn't help it. The gentlemen were so nice and understanding. We all talked for a while, and I explained to them where we were, what had happened to us, and that we had lost everything. We didn't even have clothes. They wanted to do everything that they could to help us out. They ended up giving us a hundred-dollar gift card to Walmart where we could go by ourselves some clothes.

I just started crying even more but with happiness because they cared and they showed they cared. They gave all of us a hug, told us how sorry they were, and said that if we needed anything to let them know and they would see what they could do to help.

The insurance company had called and said they would be out the next day. It was getting on out into the late afternoon hours anyway.

So we all decided that we would call it a day. I told the kids I didn't know how long we were going to be separated because I still didn't know where all of us would stay to be together. We couldn't all stay in the camper because it wasn't big enough for all of us.

Ro'chele went back to her friend's house, and the boys stayed on at the camper. I went back to Daddy's. What was crazy was that Ro'chele's friend lived in a trailer also and the tornado had done a lot of damage to it as well, but they had some friends who had a house that they could stay in. It was good that she had a place where she could stay comfortably.

The next day, Daddy and I got up early and got ready to go up to the property to meet the insurance adjuster about the house. I was hoping that he would get there early, and we wouldn't be sitting there waiting all day long on him. But the day did fly by pretty quickly because while we were waiting on him, our auto insurance company sent out a roll-back truck to pick up our vehicles.

It just depended on your auto insurance, but our company had so many claims that they were having to pick up the vehicles and take them to a secured place until they could get adjusters out to assess everyone's damage. They had to drag my car out of the trees on its side. It was unreal to sit there and watch what they had to do in order to get the vehicles out. But they had to do what they had to do, and it was not like it was going to do any worse damage than what they already had.

The gentleman finally got my car dragged out of the trees, and then he had to get it flipped over where he could load it up on the roll-back. It took him a little over an hour to get it out and loaded. Then I had to sign the paperwork stating the wrecker company had picked up our vehicles for our insurance adjuster and issued an identification number for the car. It was a pretty neat system though and smart at that. It also kept the customers from having to wait weeks upon weeks or possibly even months to get their insurance checks.

After he got mine loaded, Derrell had to follow him down the road to where his truck was down in a field. We all went to go watch. I didn't stay long because I needed to be at the property in case the home-owner's insurance adjuster got there. It wasn't too long after we got back that he drove up, so it was a good thing that I came back when I did.

I greeted him as he got out of his car and introduced myself and my dad. He walked around for a minute. He took maybe two pictures and turned around and told me what he was going to do. He already knew what he was going to do before he had even seen what was left, which was nothing. I was in complete shock when he started explaining everything. He had basically done what they called a "forced mortgage," which meant that they completely paid your mortgage off but you had no money to replace anything that you lost—no money for a hotel room, for clothes, for food, and most of all nothing to replace your old home to have a roof over your head.

I was so angry, confused, and hurt. I had tears rolling down my face as I turned around and asked him what I was supposed to do about getting us a new home, and he basically said that wasn't their problem. If I would have had a baseball bat and if I would have been able to have swung it with my left arm, I probably would have knocked his windshield out. But then again, what good would that have done? None. I might have felt better for getting a little anger out, but he wasn't worth it.

I stood in the driveway, crying and crying as the insurance adjuster left. I absolutely could not believe that he was so heartless. He stood there and saw nothing was left and that I had been injured, and he still had no remorse whatsoever over his decision. That is one lesson that I have learned about insurance. Read the fine print. Because somewhere in that declaration, they don't cover something and you'll hear about that later on in the book.

It had taken a little longer to get Derrell's truck on the roll-back than it did my car. The truck had gotten stuck in the field trying to get to his truck. They had to bring a tractor over to help try to get the roll-back unstuck, but the ground was still so saturated from all of the storms and rain that we had that anything would get stuck. They finally got it out, and the kids came on back down to the property.

Derrell was going to take his buddies' tractor down the road and help some of the neighbors move some trees and debris. Ro'chele helped out neighbors by picking up debris and sorting through things that were pieces left of people's lives. It made them feel better to be able to help others. It was our community, and we all were coming together as a family to pitch in and help one another the best we could.

A week had not even passed, and it was absolutely unbelievable watching people from just about every state it seemed like coming in to assist us. The power trucks were from everywhere. Crews had traveled down to get power lines back up. Just a few of the states that sent their power trucks were Tennessee, Kentucky, North Carolina, Georgia, and Florida. I mean they were coming from everywhere. It was just amazing. Those guys came in and had new lines and power back going within a week's time. They worked from dusk to dawn, running chainsaws and anything else they had to do. They were there to help their neighbors, and they did just that.

Then area community centers and churches from everywhere were bringing in supplies: water, food, clothes, blankets, tarps, batteries, mosquito repellant—you name it, they were bringing it. Our community center in the valley had opened their building and even started cooking for all of the people in the valley along with feeding all of the volunteers to show how much we appreciated people caring for us. Usually, your small towns get left out and are not always as important as your big towns.

Everyone came together as one big family and did whatever they had to do to help one another out. With the protection that we had from our county deputies, looting was very minimal. And even if we would have had any looters, everyone in the valley would have taken care of the others and eliminated it very quickly.

The Church of Christ churches came together from all different states and started shipping in supplies. They ended up opening up the old Liberty building where they would have a place to put everything. The old Liberty building was where they used to make Liberty overalls and jeans and so forth. So we were very blessed that they were able to use that building to store supplies because they even had companies donating furniture and mattresses for people.

It was so overwhelming to see the supplies that were being sent. We had people giving brand-new wheelbarrows, shovels, rakes, and even weed eaters. There was so much that was being donated for the community, it is hard to remember everything. They had plenty of food, shoes, clothes, towels, bathing supplies, and diapers, and they made sure we had plenty of drinking water.

I have never seen so many hundreds upon hundreds of stacked drinking water cases in my life. But our water system was down for a little while, and even when they got it back functioning, they were still telling people to be on the safe side and not use it for drinking or cooking purposes just yet. They still needed some time to get all of the lines flushed out, and it was going to be time-consuming. Everyone understood. You heard no complaints from any of us in the valley. We were just glad to get help coming in.

I had never seen so many volunteers in my life. These people came from everywhere to help. They brought all kinds of equipment—you name it, they brought it in to help people clean up debris. They even helped go through belongings that were found to get them back to their rightful owners. It was amazing to see so many caring individuals.

God definitely was watching over us and sent the people He knew that we all needed, people who cared, people who took the time to listen when we wanted to talk. They even cried with us. There were even some volunteers you couldn't get to take a cold bottle of water from you. Instead, they would always say, "We brought our own, and we also brought some more for you, because you need it more than we do." These people were absolutely God-sent people. They were complete strangers but full of love for others.

One thing about my property was there wasn't a lot of cleanup at all. All of our personal belongings and the house were completely gone. We had trees down and cinderblocks left that were under the house, but as far as shoes, clothing, pictures, and anything of that nature, we had nothing. It just disappeared. What amazes me is that I had four metal A frames, huge A frames that were in the house, and we never found one of them. So that tells you right there how powerful that tornado was.

If I would have not gotten my kids and myself and the people that were staying with us out of that house when I did, we would have been dead. I don't even think anyone would have found any of our bodies anywhere close by. After seeing the area pictures, I knew there was not much telling where we would have ended up. We are very blessed.

Volunteers continued coming in to help, week after week, until everyone received help with cleanup and removal of debris. They continued bringing in supplies to help us because there were so many of us who had nothing left. We as a community, for the most part, were still in shock. We would have people ask us what they could do to help, and all we could say was, "I don't know."

Our community started having individuals from everywhere who were trying to donate cash to certain organizations to go specifically to Shoal Creek Valley. One of the organizations was actually run off and told they were not welcome and the valley did not need their assistance when a lady who was going to donate four hundred dollars to Shoal Creek Valley was told that they could not guarantee that the money would go to Shoal Creek and that it would go where they saw fit. She grabbed her check and ripped it up. She said, "I will find another way to get those people this money." After that, the community basically ran them off and told them not to come back. But that was really the only downfall that we had to deal with at that time. There were more obstacles that did come our way later though.

I want you to understand that things are not always what they are advertised to be. I guess what I am saying is this: for example, you see this wonderful commercial on television of a certain store having a huge sale on let's say computers and you're expecting this wonderful laptop set up like a Dell computer, but when you get there, it's actually this tablet that's half the size of a piece of paper. Well, these obstacles were the same thing. Don't believe everything that you see on television because it's not what you think. I hope I haven't confused anyone, but you'll understand as you read further.

My daughter had called me on my cell phone, and she was so excited. "Momma! Momma! I found us a place to live for a while."

My mouth hit the floor. I said, "What are you talking about?"

She said, "Get Pawpaw to bring you up here where I am staying. I have already called Derrell and Chase and told them that we have a home for a while."

From a parent's personal experience, I advise you never to underestimate your children. But I have always been told that I have raised three wonderful, respectful, and caring children and they would do anything for their kids or grandkids to be the way mine are. I would always tell them, "Well, my boys always told me that I would make the best drill sergeant ever." But I am very proud of my children.

I got Daddy after he had gotten off work to take me up to meet Ro'chele, and we looked at the house. It was right next to our close friends from the valley. Their daughter and Ro'chele had been very close friends for a long time. They watched after each other and took care of one another. There were a lot of times that they were completely inseparable. They took vacations together; you name it, they did it.

Ro'chele had to have complete ACL reconstruction surgery to her right knee in 2007, and she was right there with her the whole time. I would have had my hands full sometimes if she had not been there for her because we went through this I-give-up stage and then an it-hurts-too-bad-for-therapy period. That was when we decided to throw her into my dad's swimming pool for therapy. Can you say smooth sailing? Between her best friend not letting her give up and the pool, we made it through it.

A friend of our friends from the valley had a house right next door to the one that they were staying in; it had been on the market to be sold for about a year and had not sold yet, so she called her realty company and told them about us and that she was going to let us stay there for a little while until we could get back home in the valley.

Another prayer answered. I had not even met this other family, but they took us in under their wings. They wanted to help, and this was the way they wanted to do it. They were not going to have it any other way. I had tears. I just cried and cried again. I couldn't believe it. My baby girl had found us a place to stay where we could have our family back together again. She couldn't take all of us being separated any more either. I was speechless again.

We went in and saw the house. It was so beautiful and amazing. There was beyond enough room for all of us. It was huge. It was a four-bedroom, two-bath house with a huge kitchen and a dining area, living room, laundry room, and garage, and the front and back porches went completely around the house. It was such a comfortable country-living home, but I didn't really care what it looked like as long as I could get back together with my children. It was a huge blessing.

I had to get what things I had from my dad's—which consisted mostly all of my medications—but we decided since it was so late in the evening that we would get all of us together and get moved in the following day. My son had a friend who let him use his car and then also a close friend and family of the kids had a car to let them use. I couldn't drive with my injuries but was very grateful that the kids had a way of going because they were going to have to do everything for a while. I was completely helpless and was going to be lucky to figure out how to take a shower and dress myself without any help.

Our friends from the valley were able to salvage most of their belongings, and the house that they were staying in was completely furnished so they brought their furniture over to the house we were going to be staying in. We had living room furniture, a television, and beds to use. It was just such a blessing from God.

We had all just gotten into the house, and the next thing we knew the doorbell was ringing. We were in more shock. There were friends of ours from Springville, Alabama, who had brought us just boxes upon boxes and bags after bags of everything from dishes, towels, and silverware to clothes and shoes. You name it, and they brought it to us to have. I couldn't thank them enough.

I had people actually tell me, "Please don't thank me. This is what we wanted to do to try to help. We wish we could do more." We had people bringing us blankets and bathroom necessities. The company my ex-husband worked for even gave us a washer and dryer and clothes. You name it, they sent it. I couldn't and wouldn't sleep in the bed for a very long time. I was too scared to. I was afraid to be too far from my children. So I slept on the couch where I could be close to them by their bedrooms.

Some of my coworkers came to visit and check on all of us. They had taken up donations of different items, such as pillows, blankets, and even money to help us. I had coworkers who even donated some of their sick time to me to keep a paycheck coming in because they knew that it would take several weeks for my short-term disability to kick in. They all knew that we had lost everything and needed as much help as possible.

My daughter's youth minister came by one evening and checked on us. Ro'chele was going to one church, and I was going to another when I had time to go. The work schedule that I had kept me from going to church most of the time. He asked me if I could think of anything that we needed, and I told him we had lost our Bibles. We all needed Bibles. It wasn't even a week later, and we all had new Bibles. My only hope was God, and I had to stay close to Him or I would give up and I knew that.

My daughter's softball team had taken up money and had gone and bought her all brand-new clothes. I thought that was one of the sweetest things. They also held a softball tournament for her and raised money. They had the local newspaper come up during this event, take a picture, and do a write-up on the event. It was a pretty awesome thing that they did for her. All the players even had her softball number put on the side of their helmets. I hated that she was not going to be able to finish the season out with her teammates, but with her head injuries, she couldn't do much of anything.

Ro'chele tried to go back to school, but it was very difficult on her. She had lost hearing in one of her ears from the pressure from the tornado and was constantly having headaches from the concussion and skull fracture. We ended up having her CT scans done over just to be on the safe side. She shouldn't have been having such bad headaches. They discovered that she had a small bleed from the fractured skull and that was causing all the pressure and the headaches.

She tried several times to return to school but between the hearing loss and the devastation that we all had gone through, it was just impossible for her to be able to finish what couple of weeks they had left in school. I ended up just calling the school and having them average her school grades up and just called it a year. She had great grades so she wasn't going to be affected by not passing a class or anything, and on top of that, everyone completely understood.

We all started having doctor's appointments that we had to return to for our injuries. Derrell had twenty-two staples in his back. We nicknamed him Zipper. Whatever had cut him had cut him in two lines one underneath the other. It missed his spine by a half of an inch. But it had been a couple of weeks, and it was time for the staples to come out.

Chase had stitches and pieces of wood that looked like it had come off of two-by-four pieces of plywood deeply lodged in his arm. He had a shoulder injury from lifting that power pole off of a close friend after the tornado. He kept telling the doctors about the wood in his arm, and they kept doing x-rays to come back and say, "Well, we don't see anything." He ended up having it removed in the doctor's office after about three months. The wood had finally started trying to come out on its own, and that was how they found it. It was very painful, and I felt so bad for him because it was like no one wanted to listen to him about it being in there to begin with.

Ro'chele had her stitches removed from her forehead from the glass that had lodged in her head. She had to go back and have another hearing test done. The doctors felt like it was going to be a temporary thing, but to this day, she still can't hear out of that ear. They would not stitch or staple up the back of her head where she had that huge cut. They wanted it to heal from the inside out. It is still very tender, and she is still constantly having glass that eventually works its way out of her head.

I do understand why they wouldn't staple or stitch certain wounds. I mean, there wasn't much telling what kind of dirt, rocks, and debris were still inside the wounds. All the doctors wanted any of us to do was keep the areas cleaned, apply the medications they prescribed, and keep them covered so eventually everything that possibly was left in the wounds would work its way out as the wounds were healing from the inside out.

We were all just very impatient and wanted everything to heal overnight so we could get on with our lives, but it just didn't happen that way. We all took a big beating, and it simply took our bodies a lot longer to heal. We all still hurt to this day from our injuries. When it rains, we all know. When it starts turning colder, we all know. There are just some injury side effects that we are all going to have to live with. They will definitely remind us that we had been injured and survived an EF4 tornado.

My mother and sister took me to my first back-to-the-doctor visit. I knew I was going to have to have my daddy for a lot of other doctor visits because Mother and my sister were only allowed so much time off, and then they still had to make up that lost time. But anyway, we ventured on down to UAB Highlands because they were going to remove the cast that I had along with the staples and check out the other wounds.

They took x-rays first. Even though I had a cast on, with such advanced technology, they could do that now. Then we went to the casting room. They removed the cast. I was feeling sick at my stomach already because I still had broken bones. The reason for the plate and screws was to hold the bones together and hopefully eventually they would completely heal. But the technician began removing the last bit of wrapping. He was carefully looking at my arm.

My surgeon came in and took a look at things. He tried to reassure me that everything was looking the way it was supposed to. I had twenty-six staples in my arm. I had twenty-two stitches in my elbow, and I had pins in my wrist stabilizing it. The pins had these colored balls on the ends of them, but they were not ready to remove those just yet.

He started removing the staples one by one, and I was getting sicker and sicker at my stomach. These were and always will be the doctor's famous words: "It's not going to hurt. You may feel a little tug, but that's all." Well, I was ready to tug him. Yes, it hurt. No, it wasn't just a tugging feeling. I'm not going to lie to you.

I began getting dizzy as he was pulling more and more of the staples out. I was fixing to pass out. My mother and sister knew that something wasn't right because they saw me when I started sweating and I turned white as a sheet. I told that technician that I had to lie down or I was fixing to fall out on him.

I lay down on the table a few minutes, and he came back and checked on me. He stated that we had to continue. We could hurry up and get everything removed, and then I would feel better. I just stayed there lying back and let him go for it. There was no way that I could sit back up. It hurt worse as he was coming further up my arm. I just kept thinking to myself, *Please hurry, and let's get this through with. You have no idea how this feels.* He finished with the staples and then removed the stitches.

My surgeon came back in and looked at my arm after everything had been removed. He needed to make sure that everything was sealed and nothing was going to pop back open, and then we had one more thing we had to do. He was putting me back in a cast. So I was back at the beginning, where we started.

I still was not going to be able to do anything. It was a lot harder on me because I was dominant right-handed. Then he said, "I will see you back in six weeks."

I was like, "You're kidding. Six more weeks?"

"Yep, six more weeks."

At the time, I didn't fully understand my injuries anyway. He also told me that if I were to hit the cast down at my wrist area accidentally that I would know it because of the pins. He warned me to be careful and to make sure that I didn't get the cast wet. I was also to keep my arm elevated all the time in order to get the swelling to start coming down because I had a lot of swelling still. I was sitting there thinking, *Well, yeah, I just have broken bones everywhere in my arm; of course, I am going to have swelling.* I was trying to be nice even though I wanted to hurt him as he was removing the staples.

We left the doctor's office and headed back toward the house we were staying in. We went by the Liberty building and picked up a few supplies that we needed. I was just so overwhelmed by all of the people who were helping our community. We had endless supplies of necessities that just kept coming in from different states.

We had gone by the post office to pick up our mail. They were holding everyone's mail for them until everyone could get situated. With all of the cleanup, power trucks, and huge debris removal trucks, the post office decided that it would be best if they just held the mail and we could go by and pick it up. We were all grateful for that service as well. We didn't have to worry about people taking advantage of us and stealing our mail during the middle of the night.

Of course, I couldn't cook or clean or do anything. Ro'chele's church, Ashville First Baptist Church, started organizing a food bank for us, and they had volunteers who would cook us supper and bring it to us. I thought that was the most thoughtful thing. God laid our family on their hearts, and that was just the beginning of His plan for us. I enjoyed seeing and talking with all of the different people from the church. It helped my heart a lot, and you will understand why I say this further along in the book.

I finally received mail from the home-owner's insurance company and the mortgage company. It was the biggest nightmare of my life. I started receiving letters every day. They would state that I could not do anything with the remains of the home. Well, I was sitting there wondering, *What remains?* Then I received a letter stating that they had done the forced mortgage and paid the balance off from the mortgage and that we would not be receiving any money to replace the home or its contents.

It started hitting me hard again when I received that letter. I cried and cried because I absolutely did not know what I was going to do. The kids kept telling me that it would all work out and to stop worrying because we would figure something out. They told me that I couldn't get better worrying and things happen for a reason.

I knew deep down in my heart that things happened for a reason, but this was just too much for one person to take in at once. I felt furious and even asked God, "Why us?" I knew you were not supposed to question things, but it was just hard not to. I couldn't understand any of this. I didn't want to understand because it just wasn't supposed to be happening.

Then I received this letter from the insurance company telling me that it was my responsibility to get rid of any and all salvaged materials left from the destruction. Then I thought, *Well, I wish I could find something. I would take it to the scrap yard where we could have some money for a home.* What was so frustrating was these people absolutely did not understand that there was nothing to be found. Our home, our belongings, our life had just vanished within forty seconds.

It would have been nice if they would have been more understanding and caring than what they were. But they didn't care. We were a number on their list, and that was all that we were. There was no "I am so sorry that you had to go through this type of devastation, and if you and your family need anything, please let us know where we can help." There was none of that. We were just a number.

Then there was this one letter from the insurance company that was something else. They sent me this nice letter stating that they had completed their inspection of the property for damage due to a recent hurricane. I said, "What? A *hurricane*!" These people had lost their minds. So I got on the phone with them for them to inform me that they had no underwriters for tornadoes because we were considered Tornado Alley and that was why it stated "hurricane" because of the 185-mile-per-hour-plus winds.

Well, I lost it with them. I told them that was not going to work and that they were going to have to rewrite that letter because I would not be able to get any assistance since they stated it was a hurricane. Then I was going to have to come up with more proof that I lived there and owned the property. Then I reminded them that I had lost all of those documents and unless they were going to pay for me to get those documents back, they needed to figure something out and fast. What little patience I had was running very thin with them.

The following day, I received a letter stating that it was my responsibility to protect the property from any further damage. I thought to myself, *Now tell me. Just how do you manage that one? I can't control what the weather does.* There was nothing left to protect. We had no trees left. We had nothing. I was almost at my breaking point—or that was what I thought at the time.

I received the final letter a week later stating that they had declared my home a total loss and that they were sending such amount of a check to me to sign over to the mortgage company. Once I received the check, I had twenty-four hours to endorse it and send it to them. I didn't have a problem with that at all. It wasn't like I could cash the check and leave the country with the money. I mean the check was made out to me and the mortgage company. Without their signature as well as mine, the check was no good. Along with this letter, they decided that they would cancel the insurance and that they would not cover the property or anything else. They had done their part, and they were finished.

The lesson learned was this: please read your policies. There are always stipulations somewhere unless you ask questions. They are not going to offer any more than what they have to. Most companies offer only basic things. For example, I found out later that my policy, if I were to, say, have my water heater to go out during the day while I was at work and flood the whole house and the floors would have to be replaced, they would not have covered it. It would not be considered under the flood policy that I was paying for.

I now have a great home-owner's insurance company. They took the time to explain every detail of every question that I had and I am covered for anything. I decided to go with the same company that I have my auto insurance with. I knew those people very well, and they treated me like I was human.

They cared about everything that we were having to go through. They listened when we needed to talk, and they completely understood why I was asking so many questions. They even offered to help us in any way that they possibly could. They cared, and that was what counted. Also, there was no fine print, hidden things like the other insurance company had, and they were local, so that made a huge difference.

I was about ready to pull my hair out by the time I got through with the previous insurance company. Then I had to deal with the wonderful mortgage company. Round two...ding, ding. It was like we were in a boxing ring or something. No matter how many times I explained myself to these people, they continued to call every day. I had one girl tell me she was fixing to come knock on my front door. I told her if she could find it, to please let me know.

The mortgage company started hounding me because, for some reason, the insurance company's check was not enough to pay the mortgage off. I was so frustrated. It just seemed like it was one thing after another. No one considered that we were victims and needed a chance to get everything figured out and get help. They didn't care. They didn't care that my family was in the actual tornado and was severely injured. I never in my life would have thought that being a victim of a natural disaster would be so complicated. I always just thought that if you had insurance, you were covered. I always thought that other organizations just gave you what you needed right then and there. I never thought that it was so difficult to prove that you were a victim.

My sister would come up every weekend to help me. My mother worked a second job on the weekends so there were times that she couldn't come, but she did what she could. The company that my sister and mother worked for during the week started taking up donations for us. They would send clothes, Bibles, and money. They had taken up so many different things, I don't remember everything that they sent to us. It was just so heartfelt, especially with everything that I was having to deal with between the insurance and mortgage companies.

All that I needed at that time was people just to show that they cared and that their prayers were with me. I was so at the edge of giving up, but I knew I couldn't because of the children. I was trying not to show my weakness to anyone. It was beginning to be hard though. I had more on my plate than I could handle alone, and my sister knew that. So she made sure that she came up every weekend to sort through the letters and see if I was missing anything.

Between the pain and medications and trauma, I could not think. I could not make decisions. At times, I didn't know who I was or why I was existing. I kept asking God why He didn't kill me when He had a chance. Why did He think I was good enough to survive if I was still being tortured?

My sister was at a standstill with helping me as far as paperwork was concerned because until we heard something from FEMA, there wasn't really anything that we could do. She continued to bring us things that she knew we needed and that people would bring to her for us. She even had this lady give her an outdoor rocking chair to give to me so I could sit on the back porch and enjoy a little sunshine.

I went through this two-week spell where I didn't even want to get out of bed. I just slept all the time because I felt so helpless. I was getting aggravated because of my injuries and not being able to function the way I wanted to. The rest actually helped me because I kept my arm elevated like I was supposed to and the swelling started coming down. I had to go back to the doctor before my six weeks because they had to put a new cast on. My arm had started moving around inside the cast because of the swelling coming down, and they didn't want that because of all of the fractures to my radius.

We went back to UAB Highlands, and this time, I decided to get a neon-yellow cast. I thought that at least if I decided to get out and go to Walmart with the kids, that surely people could see that cast and not run over me or be inconsiderate with their buggies being in such a hurry to grab things and leave. That's the problem with people; I was one of those people as well. We are always in a rush. Rush to work. Rush to the store. Rush to cook. Life is just a rush. No time to enjoy the things that God has given us to enjoy.

My sister had found out from the local news that they were actually going to offer a one-time food assistance through Food Stamps for tornado victims. She had brought the information to me, and we looked it over. I called them, and sure enough, they were. They gave us the dates, the time, and the location. We knew that I couldn't cook, but at least I could get some simple microwaveable things and snacks and drinks that would be easy and accessible for me and also easy for the kids.

Derrell had gone back to work, and Chase was still seeing doctors trying to get that wood out of his arm that they never could find until it eventually started working its way out. So I got Chase to drive me down where they were doing the Food Stamp program. It didn't take us long at all. It was the easiest thing that I had done so far, and I didn't get turned down. I was very impressed.

Derrell actually was at home from work when we got back, and I was confused because it was like noon and he didn't usually get off work until 5:00 p.m. and sometimes later. It just depended on what they were doing on the job. They had sent him home because he had to put a harness on for work and it rubbed his scar. It was tender in that area, and they would not let him return to work until he went back to the doctor and got another release for his injury.

He was furious, but I kind of understood where they were coming from. I mean for a person to survive an EF4 tornado and still have tenderness in places from injuries, being a major company, they did have to clear themselves from any possibilities of reinjury. The last thing they wanted was to end up having a workers' compensation claim. But at the same time, he already had a work release and was trying to work to get enough money up to buy himself another vehicle. None of us had a vehicle. They were all being borrowed from some of our closest and dearest friends.

He called and made himself another doctor's appointment for the following day to get a second release to go back to work. The doctor told him and stated in the letter that the tenderness from having staples was not uncommon and it was basically scar tissue that with time would harden into a coating and would not be so tender. He still has tenderness to this day, but that is just a part of life he has learned to deal with.

The kids and I went on our adventure to Walmart. I was very nervous about being out in public just yet. It was partially because of my arm, but I just wasn't ready to deal with society in general. I was so hushed-hushed in my own little world because of everything going on and what had happened that I simply was not a people person. I couldn't deal with myself much less others.

I went anyway to get out of the house a minute. I made the kids get things that they needed for lunches at work and for the house that were simple and easy for them to deal with because Momma couldn't cook right now. I made sure they got plenty of snack cakes and so forth. Ashville First Baptist Church ladies would still bring us food, but Ro'chele was such a picky eater, I made her get things like Hot Pockets and so forth that she liked. She would eat chicken and spaghetti and things of that nature, but she wouldn't eat the vegetables and home-cooked meals like the boys and I enjoyed. So we had to find a happy medium. It all worked out because she got what she wanted and the boys and I enjoyed home-cooked meals.

We began a fresh new week, and the letters started pouring in. I would have gone completely insane if not for my sister. I promise you that. We were denied assistance because I had home-owner's insurance. I was denied any medical help because I had insurance. They denied me dental assistance because I had insurance. I was denied property damage and debris cleanup because I had insurance. Oh, one other one. I was denied contents help because I had insurance.

I wanted to know why I couldn't get help. I was told it was because I had insurance. Well, yes, I had insurance but the problem was that it was a forced mortgage and I received no money. The mortgage company did. Well, prove it. Okay, I didn't have a problem with that.

I ran across my next-door neighbor, who was also trying to get help. I hadn't seen her because I would leave so early in the mornings for work and she would be coming in from work so we only waved at each other.

Well, remember that previous insurance letter that I just knew was going to cause issues because they had put that it was hurricane damage? Well, it did. I was so mad. I understand that protocols have to be followed because not all people are truthful, but this was ridiculous. It was every day of gathering more proof that I was a tornado victim.

I finally had this one gentleman who was very sincere and nice to me. He didn't act like he minded being there and doing his job. His tone of voice was very caring, and he took time with me. He looked over all my papers with me, including the home-owner's insurance papers. He explained to me that I would be able to get help. He specifically told me that even with a forced mortgage, which meant no money came directly to me, that I would get help. He explained to me that I would have to write appeal letters—or in my case, have someone write them for me. He wrote down a list of everything that I needed and what I needed to do.

I said, "Thank You, Jesus," and gave him a hug. I thanked him for his time and help and said that I didn't know what else to do.

He said, "Well, that's why we are here, to help." He gave me this smile and even asked me if we needed any water or food because there were supplies of water next door in the church that they also were using and food at the community center where people were cooking for the victims. I told him, “No, thank you,” and that he had done enough for me.

I had my hopes up so high that I was waiting for a check in the mail like the next day. It didn’t quite work that way, but I did have more hope than I had had twenty minutes prior. The letters started pouring in about a week later, and I had to have my sister’s help more than ever. With some of the letters, I just couldn’t understand what they were wanting, and with other letters, I would just say, “Really? You’ve got to be kidding.”

I wasn’t the only one who was getting denied. People from every county of the whole state were. It was part of the process that we were just going to have to deal with. Like I said before, some of it, I completely understand, but some of it, I thought was completely unnecessary. We were victims, homeless, vehicleless, and everything else. Every time I rode down the valley, I was constantly reminded of what happened on April 27, 2011.

It didn’t matter what it was. I had to send proof of medical bills and copayments that were not covered. I had to send proof of all my medications that we bought. I had to have written verification from the pharmacy showing where prescriptions had been filled and the dates. I had to send written verification from the physician who wrote the prescriptions along with written verification of being in the doctor’s office and being seen.

Then I would get letters stating that I would not get any money for personal property or transportation. Well, the gentleman I previously told you about told us what to do on those appeal letters. I had to try to remember and list down everything that I owned from inside the home all the way to outside and even in the sheds we had. It took me a week to get close to what we might have had. I made each one of the kids sit down and write a list of things that they could remember that they had.

The transportation denial I could care less about. I had full coverage on my car. Derrell had full coverage on his truck. But we did also learn valuable information on this as well. I only had liability insurance on Ro’chele’s 4Runner, and we couldn’t find all of the paperwork that was needed for it. So we ended up eating that one. Chase had just bought his 4Runner the day before the tornado. He didn't even have time to get insurance on it much less a tag or the title changed over. It was a mess. The lesson learned was that if you wanted your vehicle replaced at whatever the value was at the time, even if it was paid off, you needed to consider continuing full coverage; otherwise, if something were to happen, they would not replace it with another vehicle. Take out gap insurance, if offered, on a new vehicle. I know it's a few extra dollars a month, but trust me, it's well worth it in the end.

My daughter was fixing to start her classes with the University of Alabama, and I had not even thought yet about the phone, Internet, cable, or anything. I was so tied up with doctors, insurance companies, and mortgage companies. I had completely forgotten that she was going to have to have Internet access to do her class work.

I called the water company and explained to them where we were and asked about having the water temporarily turned off. The woman politely told me that they couldn't do that without having to charge me a reconnect and a new meter fee later when we did get moved back home because they would have to pull the meter. I understood everything she was saying because I had worked in the water field for fifteen-plus years. But they were able just to leave it on, and since it wasn't being used, they would just bill me a minimum amount every month. I was okay with that.

I called the power company and had them transfer my service over to the house we were staying in because we had no idea how long it was going to take to get moved back to the valley. They noted the circumstances on the account and waved the transfer fees to and from and back to our usual location. They were very understanding and helpful. They even offered free water heaters to victims when they started rebuilding again. I thought that was awesome.

Next was the phone company. They came out to the house we were in and hooked up the Internet for us. I explained that I didn't need anything but the Internet so they fixed it to where if I wanted to hook up a phone that I could use it locally, but I didn't even do that. I didn't want to hear the phone ringing. I had enough to deal without people calling.

I ended up opening up a new account with Dish Network because the people who had been living with us evidently had the cable at the old house in their name. That process took a little longer with having to prove who I was and that the property was mine and that I had been at that location for twenty years. But eventually, we did get satellite. We even had them to where they would, when we got ready to move back home, do upgrades for us and transfer it back home without charging us any other fees. I thought that was very considerate of them.

Now, we were ready; if we had bad weather, at least we could watch the local weather. I did end up having a huge ordeal after about a month of having satellite turned on back in my name because evidently the people who had been living with us were trying to get satellite service as well. But the problem was they were using my address I found out later.

It was such a huge mess that I ended up having to fax proof to the main company proving who I was, where I was at the time, and that the property was mine and not theirs. Talk about frustrating. I was getting angrier by the minute. They ended up having to cut all services off. I had to delete them off of my account and address and restart a brand-new service again for the second time. Also, it had to be noted that no one could use my address without written permission from me.

Well, that wasn't the only thing that happened. Our Internet got turned off and my phone had been red flagged. Why? Because again, the people who had been living with us were using my address and calling in on my account, but what red-flagged it was when they asked for verification of my Social Security number. According to the phone company, she had called five times in one day. But at least for security reasons they were paying attention, even though the Internet was turned off until I called in. They explained to me what was going on, and we got that fixed and taken care of. I mean, come on, what was up with all of this? It was my home, my property; I was just being nice.

I learned many lessons from this experience. Some have been very valuable. As the old saying goes, "Live and learn." I lived, and I was definitely learning. I told the good Lord above that He was going to have to really convict me for the next time that a situation came up to help someone out as far as staying with me. I just couldn't see me ever doing that again.

My sister and I had completed all the paperwork and all of the appeal letters that we could do. Now, I had to wait on the response letters. The wait was what took the longest. I would call them to verify that they had received all the information and they did not need anything else as far as my part was concerned. They would always reassure me that they had received everything and that it would take several weeks for processing and to get to the appropriate appeals departments.

By this time, I had another doctor's appointment. This time, they had to redo the x-rays and check on the bones to see if they were healing and also to see about removing the pins in my wrist. I was by no means looking forward to this. Remember, the last time, I had been told that it would not hurt removing the staples?

My mother had to work to make up for lost time as it was. So my dad took me to this doctor's visit and my sister met us there. Honestly, I am glad that he went with me because I needed a man's affirmative look when I was having those pins removed—in other words, a look telling me not to be a wimp because it would be over quickly.

The x-rays were showing everything they expected, and then it was time to go to the casting room again. They removed the cast with this small saw-looking thing. It sure did stink as they were cutting through the cast—like something was burning. I was getting nervous because I started feeling the pressure from the cast cutter, and the only thing that was going through my mind was, *Oh, Lord, he is going to cut my arm off.* I knew he had done this a million times before, but still the thought did occur to me.

They slowly got all the bandages off from underneath the cast. The doctor walked over and looked at everything; he told them the x-rays looked good and to go ahead and remove the pins. The technician looked at me and said, "Now, you're going to feel pressure as I pull the pins out, but it's not going to be as bad as you think. You will feel the tugging as they are coming up through your bones because we have to pull a little." Well, I had gotten a little smarter for this one. I had taken a pain pill before we had gotten to the doctor's office this time, so I was ready. Well, I thought I was anyway.

He started unscrewing one of the balls that was on the end of one of the screws. He placed that one in a container, and then he had these needle-nose pliers. That was when I decided that it was best for me not to watch. I looked over at my dad and sister. My dad gave me this nod of "it's all right." I knew right then I could show no sign of weakness.

He started pulling, tugging, and twisting. I felt it, and all I could do was grab the side of the table that I was sitting on, take a deep breath, and grit my teeth. I had sweat beads running down my forehead. I turned around with gritted teeth and all and asked him, "Can you not give me a deadening shot or something?"

"No we can't."

I almost asked him why not, but by this time, he was at the end of the pin, pulling it out, and that hurt the worst.

He told me that he would give me a minute before he started on the other one. I asked him why it was hurting so badly, and he said, "Because it doesn't take but a minute and everything starts trying to seal up where the wound was. Like someone that has a feeding tube, when it's removed, it seals up very quickly."

My wrist was throbbing. That pain pill had no effect on that kind of pain whatsoever. I was thinking, *Where is the morphine?*

He came back over after he gave me a couple of minutes to get through cursing him or whatever, and he said in a very nice tone, "Are you ready for the other one?"

I almost said, "What do you think?" But he was being nice to me, so I wasn't going to be sarcastic to him. I gritted my teeth and nodded my head yes. I was trying to get myself braced for this one. The ball looked bigger this time, so I figured it was going to be worse than the first one.

Then again, I didn't know if it was a different size or not because my vision was a little blurred, but it felt no different. Actually, this one did hurt worse. He started pulling, tugging, and twisting, and I started praying, "Lord, help this man hurry and get this one out, because I am about ready to pin him." I started sweating, and my stomach was getting upset. I was like, "Okay, mister, you either hurry or we are going to have a disaster."

I kept telling him the closer that he got to pulling the pin out to shove it back in. It hurt too much. I looked over at my dad and sister and said firmly while I was gritting my teeth that I was sorry but this was a little painful. It wasn't about strength. It was about he better hurry up if he wanted to live. That was how bad it was. I still didn't understand why they couldn't deaden that area.

He finally got it removed, and for a second, I felt a relief, but then it started throbbing. They put a splinted brace on my arm and told me that I needed to go to therapy in the next room. I was like, "Great. Do I have to?"

"Yes, you have to if you want to relearn how to use your arm and wrist." That kind of got my attention a little bit. I had a lot in store for me, and I was clueless about any of it. I was already getting impatient with the situation and not being able to do anything or depend on myself like I wanted.

My sister went on back to work, and we went on in to therapy. We sat there a few minutes and my wrist was about to kill me. I couldn't take another pain pill because it was too early. It wasn't too long before they called my name over to do a little therapy and to discuss my occupational therapy sessions that I was going to have to have and how many times a week.

The therapist removed the brace and began carefully looking over my arm and wrist and reviewing the doctor's notes. We had to start at a very slow pace. She explained to me that I had to start moving my fingers slowly, so I attempted that process. We did a few other things, for example, like trying to flip my arm over, which was not happening, and seeing if I could move my wrist at all yet, and that wasn't happening either.

She was going to have to put this "sock" over my arm that had an opening for my hand to go through. To me, it looked like an ace bandage with a hole cut in it. But she started sliding it over my hand up onto my arm, and I started crying because it hurt so badly. This burning sensation was running up through my arm, and she ended up removing it because it was too painful. The purpose was to help with the swelling and to keep it from moving. It was also easier to put the brace on and take it off.

She got the brace back on, and I had no intention of removing it. The doctor wanted me in occupational therapy three times a week for several months. I explained that there was no way that I could get back and forth to Birmingham three times a week. The doctor still would not let me drive, and I had to depend on people to help me.

We started looking down the list of therapists because I couldn't use just any. For some reason, the name Rhetta jumped out at me, and she was also in Moody, Alabama, which was very close to Ashville, so I asked about her. The other therapist told me that I could use her and that she was very good. So they wrote me the prescription for therapy with Rhetta.

I got my dad to run me by the post office on the way home from the doctor's office. I had letters on top of letters in the mail. The mortgage company had sent me like three letters back to back, and then I had about ten other letters from different organizations. I thought to myself, *Well, this is going to be an exciting evening sorting through all this mess.*

Needless to say, I didn't get to look at the mail. I was hurting so badly that I couldn't do anything except take my medications and go to bed. The kids had bought me this L-shaped pillow, and it really came in handy. The doctor failed to tell me that I was going to be in severe pain for a few days. Once Daddy got me back home and situated in bed, I did not move.

I was hurting so badly that by the time the kids got home, I was in tears. I couldn't get my arm elevated just right to stay out of pain. With enough medications, I finally fell asleep for a while. The kids would constantly come in and check on me. I made the mistake of moving, and I started screaming because it hurt so much.

I ended up staying in bed for three days straight. The kids would bring me something to drink and eat and basically feed me, and then they would have to help me to the bathroom. If I moved a hair, my wrist and arm would put me in such pain that I would get sick at my stomach. The doctor told us that the pain was from the holes trying to seal back up and also bone marrow was reproducing in that area. I thought those three days were never going to pass.

I didn't open any of the mail that I had received until the end of the following week. I didn't feel like dealing with anyone, and I sure couldn't get up out of bed. So, when the kids would go get the mail, they would just put it all in a pile until I felt like looking at any of it. I was in such pain I couldn't think, so it would have done me no good even to have gotten the kids to look at it for me. It just kept piling up until the following week. I looked at it this way; it wasn't going anywhere.

I finally started going through the mountain of mail that had accumulated. Well, the mortgage company said in their letters that I owed them five thousand eight hundred dollars on a balance that the home-owner's insurance company did not cover. I threw my hands up. I was so frustrated I began crying and kept crying. I was officially at my breaking point.

I was at the house alone. Derrell and Chase were at work, and I am not sure where Ro'chele had gone. I just started pacing back and forth in frustration. I went outside onto the back porch and was sitting in the rocking chair that had been given to me for a little while. I was so overwhelmed with this whole situation that I couldn't sit still.

I finally just completely broke down. I started praying out loud and having this huge discussion with God. I had no choice. I knew that God wanted me and was waiting this whole time for me to finally give it all to Him. And that was exactly what I did. I said, "God, I don't know what else to do. I have done everything that I possibly could and some. I have gathered and given everything that these people have requested, and it still has not been good enough. It is in Your hands from now on. My way is not working, and I have no other choice but to hand it all over to You. If it is meant for me and my children to live in that valley and for me to finish raising my children there, then You will make a way for us to return home. If not, then it was not meant for us to be in that valley. I can't do any more than I have already done. Father, I hand it over to You. It is no longer my problem."

I could feel that God was standing next to me and listening to me. All He had been waiting on this whole time was for me to give it to Him. But instead, I continued to try to conquer it all. When I finally hit my knees and gave God all my problems, I actually felt so much better, like this huge burden had been lifted straight off of me.

The ladies from Ashville First Baptist Church continued to bring us food and to check on us every day. I actually became very close to Sondra. I had known of her for years but wasn't really close to her. She started coming over all the time, just to see how we all were doing and to check in on Ro'chele and see how she was handling everything. The youth group that Ro'chele was involved in was concerned about her because she had not started coming back to church yet, but at the same time, they completely understood because of what we were going through.

I didn't start therapy until after July 4. I was not ready to go through any more pain than what I was already going through. Mother, my aunt, and my sister and her family had come up, and they had cooked. We spent a little family time together, and it also gave my sister time to read all the letters that I had received so she could see what else we had to do.

She was as frustrated at the situation as I was, if not more. She was really mad at the mortgage company. She was ready to call the news media and even go by the office because of the guy who kept calling and being so hateful. We ended up having to write letters to the main company requesting more information on the balance. Most of it was since the insurance company didn't completely pay it off in full, it was charging me interest by the day on the unpaid balance.

We ended up getting them to settle out for the balance owed to be $2,500. We had them remove the interest because legally, they couldn't do that and then the actual balance that was left was from a couple of years prior, I had to get an extension on the mortgage around Christmastime. I could see having to pay that but not all that interest that they kept trying to add on to something that no longer existed.

The FEMA letters were basically just letting us know that we did not have to send any more information to them, that they had everything that they needed and now it was up to the appeals officers, and that it could take a few weeks to process everything because of the number of people who had filed for FEMA assistance. I was just relieved that we didn't have to send anything else. I promise you, we had faxed them close to a hundred different letters and proof of everything from the house being destroyed to medical bills and prescriptions. You would think that eventually my claim file folder was pretty much overflowing with paperwork. We gave them everything that they asked for and then some.

The following week, I started therapy with Rhetta, who ended up being a close and dear friend of mine after months upon months of therapy. I had to go to therapy for so long that we had to get approval from the health insurance company for more therapy because I needed it in order to get some movement out of my arm and wrist.

The good Lord knew whom I needed for therapy when He kept having me go back to Rhetta. She was the best. When I met her on the first day of therapy, she reviewed all of the doctor's notes from my surgery and was so sympathetic about the whole situation. She hated that I had been injured and was having to go through what I was going through, and she was so glad that we lived through it to tell the story about what we went through and what it took to be a survivor.

Rhetta started very slowly with my therapy, and I am so glad. She wanted to cover every aspect of the area with my wrist and arm to try to get the most movement and usage out of it possible. I had a shoulder injury as well. It took a while to get everything to start loosening up since I had been in a cast for four months.

She knew the very first day of therapy what it was going to take to get some usage out of my arm and wrist. She knew that not only was she going to have to do a lot of work to help me, but I was also going to have to be determined and not get frustrated about the process and the outcome. I came into therapy with an open mind and determination to get back to work, and she knew that. It helped her learn my frame of mind, and she knew right then that I wasn't going to be one of these people who wanted a pity party. I was there to get better. It made her job a lot easier. Trust me. She told me herself.

I felt so bad for her though on that first day. Bless her heart. She was trying to put one of those "socks" on my arm, and it just wasn't happening. I screamed bloody murder and was crying and crying. She told me right then that the burning sensation that I was having was nerve damage. I kept apologizing to her and even to the other patients, but I couldn't control the pain. Rhetta was really hoping that it wasn't going to be as bad as what we later discovered as we went along the way through therapy.

It was something that neither one of us could do anything about, but I still needed to stay focused on the determination that it was going to take to get through this. She always kept a positive frame of mind even though she knew deep down inside that I would probably never have the same usage as I had before the tornado with my arm. That was what kept me going. It was her inspiration, the hope that she gave me, the caring as an individual.

After a few sessions, I started opening up to her and talking more to her because I felt comfortable. She was there to help me physically, but she also helped me mentally. I was able to ease my mind off of the things she was having to do to actually get a little movement out of my wrist and hand by talking to her.

I would go to therapy three times a week, and every day that I would go, I would go with more and more determination to get back to being like I was before. Every time I would have to go back to the doctor, she would always do my measurements and her notes for the doctor so he could see where we stood and the accomplishments that were being made through therapy.

We both worked so hard at every session to keep striving forward. My goal was to get back to work. We spent many months, step-by-step, exercise by exercise, to get the movement that I have today. She made me some special splints as we got further into therapy to help bend my wrist backward and forward. She spent many endless hours even after she got home from work, just thinking about what else we could do for therapy.

There were times that I would push myself so hard that I would be very sore after therapy. Rhetta just kept inspiring me and explaining to me that it was going to be sore sometimes but I also had to do therapy at home on the days that I didn't come to see her. She printed off a bunch of exercises for me and made me different gadgets to use as well.

This was the kind of person she was. She sent her receptionist to Walmart one day during therapy. She took the money out of her own pocket to invest in one of those exercise balls for me to have at home.

Rhetta was a very down-to-earth and caring person. She wasn't just my occupational therapist; she was my close, dear friend.

When we got closer to the end of therapy, she had to do some tests for the doctor, such as my weight-bearing capacity—what I could lift, the pounds, and if I was steady or shaky. Some of them were a little difficult, but she still kept the hope there for me. She completed all of her paperwork for the doctor and reviewed it with me. I was still determined to get back to work. We actually both thought that the doctor would probably release me as long as I kept showing progress.

I had gone back to my doctor the following week after we had completed therapy and did all the necessary tests. My heart was broken and so was Rhetta's. The doctor refused to let me go back to work. He ended up disabling me because of the type of work that I did. He could not take a chance of me hurting myself or anybody else because I would never be able to lift the weight that I once could with my arm.

The doctor was also afraid that if for some reason my arm broke into pieces with the plate and screws in that there wasn't much more that they could do for me and it was just way too risky to let me go back to work. He ended up completely disabling me—not partially but completely. It was heartbreaking.

I was so hurt because I had worked so hard in therapy and so did Rhetta helping me get to where I was, but he would not release me. It took me awhile to get over losing my career. But I finally thought about it, the chances I would have been taking, and the possible consequences that would have come along with it if I would have injured my arm worse than what it already was. Plus, if I had hurt one of my coworkers because I couldn't hold my end of the weight, it would have killed me. The guys that I worked with were family to me and the last thing that I wanted to do was accidentally end up hurting one of them.

I still stay in touch with Rhetta as of today, not as much as I want to, but she knows that I know that she is there if I need her and vice versa. She will always be close to my heart because she took me under her wing and lifted me up mentally where I could get through the physical part that I was having to endure. I thank God all the time for sending her to me. He knew that she was what I needed, and I have been very blessed with not only a therapist but a friend as well.

I continued patiently waiting to hear back from FEMA on any possible assistance that they might be able to provide me and my children. As the days and weeks passed, I started getting closer to Sondra from Ashville First Baptist Church.

She continued making sure that we had meals every day. We became such close friends that she knew that I was getting impatient with waiting on help, and she called me up one evening and told me she was going to come by and pick me up and that we would go have a milk shake because chocolate always seemed to help soothe the mind.

I still couldn't drive, so Sondra called me one day about coming to church with her, and she came by and picked me up. I fell in love with Ashville First Baptist Church. The people were so caring and loving. And I absolutely loved Brother James's preaching. He really made you think, and he encouraged you to go and read and study the Bible.

I was up late one evening after church. I just couldn't sleep. I had been on Facebook a couple of times, and my neighbor Denise, one of the people who had helped us the night of the tornado, had sent me a friend request.

She was having one of those nights too, and she IM-ed me. We began talking. It was amazing to find out that we actually were so much alike. We became close friends quickly. But we both could relate to what the other was going through because she had completely lost her home as well.

At this point, we were beginning to wonder if we were ever going to be able to get back home. All of a sudden, God-given blessings started happening to both of us. We had some footwork that we both had to do, but as I said before, God had a plan.

I had a friend of mine whose sister had gotten ahold of me and told me that she had run across a foundation group that was helping tornado victims. She began our conversation by telling me, "You know, the valley is so small that everybody knows everybody's business, and I hope you don't think that I am intruding in your business, but I really wanted to get this information to you."

I told her by no means was she intruding and that I would be very grateful for any help that I possibly could get right then because I had no idea how I was going to rebuild and get back home after what the insurance company had done.

She came by the next day and gave me an application for the Hero Foundation out of Birmingham, Alabama. It was one of the best things that could have happened. I filled out the application and had a meeting with Liz who was a representative of the foundation. We discussed the process.

Liz was so sweet and caring. It seemed like every day after I fell to my knees and said, "Okay, God, it's yours. I can't handle it anymore," I was just receiving blessing after blessing. There were times when I even told God that I was not worthy of everything that He was doing, but He saw differently.

Liz and I became close friends, and before I knew it, she had gathered up money for us a gift card to Walmart to help us get things that we needed. Then she went through her own clothes and brought me clothes, shoes, and purses. You name it, she brought it to me.

God kept sending people to me that I needed. He knew that I would easily give up, but He had a different plan. God gave me hope and continued to send the inspirational people that I needed to continue. God was making me stronger, and I wasn't even aware of it until later.

Liz was determined to get us some help after I had told her everything. She was working day in and day out using all resources possible to get us as much help as she could. She had left me a few extra applications in case I knew of anyone else in the valley who needed help as well.

I got on the Internet and got a hold of Denise. I told her about the foundation, and that was when it all started coming together. The next surprise was when Sondra came over and sat me down. She said, "Stacy, we are going to get you back in a home. I have been talking to Brother James, and we are going to come up with something to get you and the kids back home."

I started having chills from the top of my head all the way to my feet, and I had tears running down my face. I was speechless. All I could do was give her a big hug. She explained to me that it was going to take some work and a little while, but God had laid my family on Ashville First Baptist Church hearts and they were going to do everything they could to help.

Denise and I had heard that United Way was coming down to the valley to have a meeting for the residents to try to aid them as well. Denise came and picked me up, and off we went to the meeting. It was absolutely not going to hurt for us to go see if it could possibly be more help for us.

Believe you me, it was another beneficial meeting. Liz had already gotten in touch with Shirley at United Way and explained everything, and we both had actually already talked with Shirley as well, but we still needed to go to the meeting.

Neither one of us had even met her. We had only talked to her over the phone, but when Liz introduced us to Shirley, we both just hugged her. Neither Denise nor I had officially gotten approved for help yet from either group, but that wasn't the point.

The point was that they cared. They cared so much that they all spent endless hours upon hours doing everything in their power to get us the help that we needed. All of their work paid off in the end. It was amazing to see the glow in the eyes of those who got the help for us.

Whenever I would hug and thank people, they would automatically tell me that they felt so good inside to be able to give and help others and that this was not about fame or fortune. It was because God had sent them to us.

I had even had one gentlemen tell me that he was from Montgomery, Alabama, and it was raining and just one of those days when he almost turned around and went home. But he told me that God started convicting him, telling him that he had to go to Shoal Creek Valley, that people were depending on him, and that he could not go back home. He told me himself that if it hadn't been for God, he would not have come.

You see—and yes, it took me awhile to realize it as well—God took a devastating situation and made it into something good. We had a lot of tests and trials, but He led us all completely in the direction that we all should be willing to go anyway.

Sondra came and picked me up a few days later, and we went to meet with some of the church members at the church. These guys ended up being my best friends as well. We were meeting to discuss house plans.

Brother James had explained to me that there had been numerous people and local churches as well as other churches from all over the place that wanted to help get us back into a home. My mouth dropped. The only thing that was running through my head was, "God, what did I do to deserve such love and blessings?" The only thing He would tell me was, "Because I love you and you are my child."

We all started discussing how much it would cost to build a house with so much footage in it. It blew my mind to know how much it cost per foot to build a house. Bob actually built houses for a living, and Gordon was a certified electrician. So they both knew what it was going to take to build a house.

I had no idea because of course I never thought about having to build a house. We discussed what it was going to take money-wise even after they took off for labor costs. We all had to have an idea of what kind of footwork we were going to have to do to make this work. Brother James would always say that God was going to make a way for us, and he knew what he was talking about because He did.

I set up a time where Brother James, Sondra, and I could meet with Liz with the Hero Foundation to see what they might possibly be able to help with. Liz was positive that we could get help, but she would have to go before a board for approval, and she also had Shirley with United Way doing the same.

A few days later, I received a phone call telling me that Gallant Fire Department wanted to come up and get the area cleaned up with a Bobcat to start getting ready to build. I was so excited. I just couldn't believe it.

We had some of the teenagers from Ashville First Baptist Church's youth group come as well, and they were picking up and moving huge tree limbs by hand and doing everything to help as well. I thought that was the best thing that they could do for Ro'chele. They kept her spirits up by showing her that they loved her and that she meant the world to them. They were there to support and help her get back home.

Gallant Fire Department had even gotten Gargus Recycling and Scrap to bring one of their huge transfer truck trailers over and drop it off for any scrap metal that they might find while doing cleanup. Some of the guys knew the owners very well, and they were so happy to be able to help as well.

By the end of the day, everyone was very tired, but the goals had been met. It was astonishing to have so many people help and not one person thought twice about it. It was just so overwhelming to see and have so many people who wanted to be there and wanted to do everything they could to help us and get us back home.

There were times when I felt all these people were more excited than I was. But I was just in shock. I had never been a person to ask for help. I had always tried to figure it out on my own. So you can imagine how overwhelmed and shocked I was. God knew how hardheaded I was, and He knew that He had to take complete control of this situation. He did just that.

I continued to go to Ashville First Baptist Church and loved it so much that I requested to have my membership transferred because I wanted to be a part of their family. I felt at home and loved it so much. It was what I needed when I needed it, and God put it all into place.

Denise and I talked every day, updating each other on any new information or whether either one of us had heard from anyone yet. The more we talked, the closer we got. She would tell me every day that she was so grateful that God brought us together.

A couple of weeks had passed, and I received a phone call from

Liz letting me know that she had talked with the board and she had also called and talked with Brother James. The board had approved to give us the help that we needed. I was shouting with joy.

Then I received a phone call from Shirley with United Way. She also had good news. She had told me that their board members had also approved so much money to go toward rebuilding us a home. I was so thrilled. I just kept yelling with joy.

I walked down to the mailbox after the mail lady had come. I had been sitting on the front porch waiting on her, and I knew about what time she dropped the mail off every day. I was crossing my fingers for something in the mail from FEMA.

Well, I did receive a couple of letters from them, and my heart was just pounding because I was so nervous about opening those letters. Everything was going so well; I was waiting for something to try to set us back.

I slowly opened one of the letters to discover that they had approved so much money for me for property loss, which meant that the money that they would be sending in the amount would have to be used specifically to replace contents that we had lost.

I was so excited that I did not hesitate to open the next letter. This one was just as good. They had approved so much money to go toward rebuilding. We had been approved for the maximum amount that they could give to help each household.

I was jumping for joy. I called Sondra and Brother James and told them about the approvals. That was all we were waiting on; we could pick out blueprints for the house and get construction on its way.

Everyone was so excited. They couldn't wait to get started. We all met at the church to pick out the blueprints for the house and discuss money. We all agreed that I needed to use the FEMA money first on building supplies and then when that ran out, we would start using the other money that had been provided by everyone else.

I called Denise and asked her if she had heard anything back from anyone yet, and she said that they had but they were having a few issues because everyone kept saying the same thing to her about appealing her mortgage as well. They told her that she should be able to get help from them because she basically had the same thing that I had, which was a forced mortgage.

The sooner she could get the appeal letters in, the sooner they would be able to all come together on decisions as far as money to help her get a house built back as well. I asked her if she wanted my appeal letters to go by as an example and told her that if she needed them, she was more than welcome to them.

She called me the next day and told me they were able to get the appeal letters done and faxed over for processing as quickly as possible. I kept praying for her and her family because they were in the same boat that I had been in, and it had been frustrating and discouraging times for them as well.

I did, however, experience another setback healthwise. Once things started calming down with all the insurance and proving that I had lost everything I ever worked for in the tornado, things began quieting down.

One day, the kids had left the house we were temporarily staying in for work or school. I had this huge house all to myself and not one single time did the phone ring from people needing more information.

I began crying and crying in a way that I did not understand. I started shaking so nervously, and all I could think of was that I was having a complete nervous breakdown. My heart would race, and I felt like I couldn't breathe.

I called both my dad and mom and told them that I needed to go to the doctor that something just wasn't right. I explained to both of them my symptoms, and I think the both of them were thinking the same way that I was. I mean, I did live through an EF4 tornado.

I called and made me an appointment with my family physician. As I met with my doctor, he began asking me a series of questions. I wasn't completely sure why he was asking these questions, but I answered anyway.

I explained to him that I had begun crying all the time, and I would just shake from head to toe for no reason. He took my vital signs, and then he said, "I need to ask you a question."

I said, "Okay."

He asked me to tell him the one thing about the night of the tornado that scared me the most.

I told him that I didn't think that I was going to find my children alive. I completely broke down with him. I kept thinking to myself,

Lord, he is going to admit me back into the hospital. He began explaining to me that these medical signs that I was having were due to trauma. He asked me if I remembered having been hit in the head or anything of that nature by debris. Of course, my response was, "You got to be kidding me, right? Do you actually think that I remember what happened at the moment of being sucked up and thrown out?"

I apologized for being so sarcastic. I did explain to him about being hit as I was attempting to get up from being facedown on the ground. He continued explaining post-traumatic stress syndrome. He said to me, "You have lived through a huge natural disaster. You have been so busy dealing with insurance companies, the mortgage company, this person, that person, and orthopedic doctors that you have not had a chance to really rest. Now that everything is calming down somewhat, your body is finally relaxing enough that your brain is now reminding you of the trauma that you have experienced."

He put me on a trauma medication along with anxiety medications and something to put me to sleep at night. He set me up for a two-week return to see him. He needed to make sure that these medications were going to work and also to do blood work and update everything in my file.

I really felt no difference with the medications. I actually started having extremely bad nightmares, and the anxiety attacks became more frequent and worse. I by no means even wanted to be around people because I didn't want them to see me the way I was. I didn't understand what I was going through and my way of thinking was, *How could I possibly expect anyone else to understand?*

The two weeks came and went quickly. I returned to my physician, and for some reason, my blood pressure had shot up through the roof. It scared the doctor so badly that he put me on a heart monitor because he was afraid that I was going to go into cardiac arrest. As I lay there, he began drawing vials upon vials of blood to run tests to see if anything would show up on my blood work. I was as scared as he was—not knowing, much less understanding what was going on. I had never had blood pressure problems in my life until then.

I began explaining to him about the nightmares that I had started having. It was always the same one. I explained to him that it was when I looked up and saw the tornado heading straight for us. About that time, some of my blood work results started coming in, and one of the tests showed that my kidneys were extremely weak from when I had been hit in the back so hard by debris.

The doctor had to completely change all of my medications and add some sedatives to control the anxiety attacks, which were causing my blood pressure to shoot up so high and also another sedative to try to keep the nightmares at a minimum and under control, or they could possibly start causing me to have mini heart attacks in my sleep. At first, I argued with him about that because in my mind, I thought I was way too young to be having heart attacks. But he explained it to me so that I actually began worrying about the situation as well. We had no choice at the moment but to do exactly what he said to do.

He had to put me on blood pressure medications as well. He explained to me that I would more than likely sleep a lot, but not to worry unless I was dreaming and having spells of remembering. At first, I was really confused. But I thought, *Hey, I am not a doctor either.* I felt like a walking pharmacy when he got through writing all the prescriptions that I needed.

The medications were actually helping and working this time. I was getting peaceful rest without waking up in a sweat in the middle of the night from the nightmares. I wasn't dreaming at all, or if I was, I didn't remember dreaming. The kids by no means liked that I was on all these medications, but they didn't understand what was going on just like I didn't. I couldn't explain it to them like the doctor could.

I had never understood "trauma" or "post-traumatic stress syndrome." But I had never taken the time to understand it much less do any research on it. I mean, I'd never had a reason too. I never thought that I would experience something of that nature or a natural disaster either.

It took several months to really get all the proper medications to work the way that they needed to work for the post-traumatic stress. I explained to my doctor that there were a lot of things that I still didn't remember about the tornado. Most of my friends and family would tell me about certain events, and he explained to me that I was blocking memory, which was normal for someone who had gone through what I had and that eventually the memory would come back.

We had started groundbreaking in August 2011, just four months after the tornado hit our community in Shoal Creek Valley. Yes, it did seem like forever at first, but that was because with all the paperwork that had to be done from the beginning—starting with the home-owner's insurance and then to everything else—it just seemed like it was taking forever. But in reality, it wasn't long at all.

They had laid out the area stakes for the house and started digging the footings and laying the block on the house the same day. The next day, they had just about all the blocks completely laid out and said they would be through by the end of the day, and they were. Those guys worked from 6:00 a.m. to late in the afternoon. They were just glad that they could help.

We had to call the health department for approval on a new septic tank installation. We couldn't use the other one that we had from the old house because it had been destroyed by the tornado. The top of it had been lifted up, and the field lines had been damaged and pulled up by the roots of a large tree that we'd had in the yard.

It took maybe two days, and they were trenching, digging, and laying field lines. They had the new septic tank installed in a day's time. I don't think those guys took a lunch break at all. They had their minds set to get in there and get busy. They had a family to get back home.

They had the walls coming up very quickly, and it was beginning to look like a home again. I was getting so excited. I would go by as much as I could to check on everyone, but between doctor visits and therapy, I wasn't able to go by every day. I actually believe that it helped them out tremendously not to have someone breathing down their necks as they were working and they were able to be more productive.

These trusses were built by D&D Truss Components. Brian Kennedy, from my church, spent many hours to get these built and shipped in just a few days.

These young men were youth volunteers from my church, Ashville First Baptist. The Bobcat and volunteers were from Gallant Fire Department. They spent a half of a day in the heat cleaning up and removing debris by hand to get ready for the rebuilding of our new home.

These girls put in a long, hot day digging up and removing debris on our property. Pictured is my daughter with two of her closest friends along with her high school boyfriend. They all worked so hard from the bottom of their hearts to get us back home in the valley.

After all the trusses were put into place, this was what my new home looked like. All of the trusses were delivered and put up on the house in one day.

This was the very first truss being placed on the roof. It took everyone to come together to get everything into place the way they wanted it and the way it needed to be.

Mr. Bob, Mr. Glenn, and Mr. Bruce from Ashville First Baptist Church lifted each truss up by hand to the gentleman on top of the new home, placing each truss perfectly into place. They all worked endless hours upon days to get our new home built.

When I was able to go by and see the progression, I would always hug everyone who was helping build this home. They just didn't understand how grateful I was for having the people to get together like they did and do all they were doing. But Bob, Gordon, and Mr. Fred wouldn't have it any other way.

They were all working as hard as they could, but at the same time, they were all taking their time and doing measurement after measurement, making sure everything was perfect. They were building this house as if they were the ones moving in. I was profoundly appreciative of the way they were doing everything.

As I was told later, a house is a piece of artwork. You do it to perfection and get the best results. I absolutely believe it and am so blessed that I had the people that I did build our home. They were all perfectionists, and I knew nothing was going to be overlooked and that they were going to take care of me.

We had so many people giving us discounts, their things, and their time to get this house built. After all the walls came up, we had a couple of days when we were at a standstill due to rain. But as soon as it stopped, everyone was back at it again.

Our lives were gradually coming back together again. Ro'chele was back in school, and it was her junior year. Seeing the kids smile again was just a blessing in itself. I could see relief and the progression of moving forward with their lives, letting this experience gradually unfold and be left behind them.

It was remarkable watching how the house was just progressing every day. They had all the walls up and the inside framed and were waiting on the trusses. I happened to go by after therapy one day, and Ms. Donna and I got behind the transfer truck that was loaded down with trusses that had my name and address on them.

I was in unbelief for a moment to see such. Then I saw Brian, whom I went to church with, there. I'd had no idea that he worked for D & D Truss Components, Inc. But he had built the trusses for the house and had them shipped on over as quickly as possible.

I took pictures of the very first truss that was placed on the house and of all the people who were there volunteering their time and strength. All were from my church. We had Bob, Gordon, Glenn, Casey, Mr. Fred, Bruce, and the list just kept going.

They all had every single truss up on that house by the end of the day, and they would be ready for the roof the next day. And they were. The next day, they were laying plywood and pounding and getting ready for shingles.

We had the shingles donated from a group that was with the volunteers from the Baptist Association, and they also were able to give us both showers for the house as well. They helped out a lot as far as cutting the costs down. Everything was so expensive that every little thing was appreciated so much.

Bob explained to me that the most time-consuming part would be the inside of the house. That was because you had to do all the electrical, plumbing, and making sure that every single inch in the house measured just perfectly. Then you could start with the Sheetrock.

We had to get the attic situated with the furnace and duct work and, most important, the insulation. We had the insulation blown in the attic. But everything still kept moving well. They actually had all told me that this house was one of the most enjoyable and smoothly built houses that they had yet done.

I still to this day say that they all enjoyed it so much because it was provided and done by the hands of God. They are all such good Christian men, who truly believe in the works of God. That is what made the difference.

A friend of mine I had gone to school with and had not seen in twenty-plus years came by the house and told me he was going to do the Sheetrock in the house. He was in and out in no time. All Sheetrock was completed except a couple of pieces, and he had that in no time and was through.

A very sweet lady I worked with—well, she was in a different department than I—called me and was so excited because her church was going to donate all the paint and whatever else they could help with. They also had professional painters who were going to come up and do all the inside painting. That was what these guys did for a living, and they wanted to help.

My daughter and I had met one of the gentlemen and his wife at Home Depot one afternoon and picked out the paint colors that we wanted in the house so they could estimate about how many gallons they would need to get ordered before they could begin painting.

While all of this was going on for us, Denise was getting ready for groundbreaking for her house. Everything had come around for her and her family. They started building her house, and it was coming up quickly as well. We were all getting excited about getting back home.

Denise and I had a time period where neither one of us had a lot of time to talk because we were having to go and pick out things we wanted for our houses. I was just amazed at everything we had to shop for.

I had a close friend, Ms. Donna, to go with me shopping and write down numbers to everything. We both had a fun time doing it. Trust me; it was very tiresome going store to store. But we made the best out of it.

We had to shop for flooring because I decided that I wanted hardwood floors through the whole house. And there are the everyday things that we all take advantage of and never think about really having to re-buy them—for example, a toilet. I never in my life had seen so many different shapes, sizes, and styles of toilets before I had to go shop for one.

Bob would give me a list and Ms. Donna and I would go on the hunt for what I liked and wanted. We spent many weeks shopping. I was really glad when we had finally bought the last cabinet doorknob because some of that stuff on the list, I had never heard of and most definitely didn't know what it was.

Everyone had set a goal for us to be back home by Christmas, if not before. I told everyone that if we got back home by Christmas, that would be the best Christmas present anyone could ever ask for. It did happen. We were back home December 15, 2011.

Bob had suggested to some of the women at church to give us a housewarming at the church. It was the best. We received so many things to help get us back on our feet and going again. We received a lot of gift cards so we could see what we needed and go get things we wanted.

Two years ago, I had wondered if there were any good people left in this world, and God definitely answered that question by sending the people that He sent to us. Like I said before, everyone we met and everyone who helped all the way back to the veterans was a blessing.

I would not have made it if God had not completely turned a bad situation into great things for my family.

Denise and her family also got moved into their new home before Christmas. They still had a little bit of work to do to the house but not much. She, just like I, wanted to get back home. She also had a lot of wonderful and caring people who came together and helped to get her and her family back into a home.

When we got moved into the house, it was just overwhelming. We had so much to organize and put into place to make it our home. I did not get anxious or in a hurry to put everything away at one time. It was Christmas. The garage was stacked and packed with boxes, but I didn't care because I had already made up my mind that I would go through a box at a time and sort and put things up slowly. Like I said, it was Christmas and the best Christmas that we had had yet.

Ro'chele and I ended up going to Walmart and buying a white Christmas tree. We didn't do a lot of decorating, only the tree. We had so many decorations that Bob and his wife had given to us, it was unbelievable. We all so appreciated it because we didn't have anything.

I told them both how much we appreciated everything that they had done for us—from getting the house built to getting us back home by Christmas. All the decorations were so heartwarming. They took us in, as if we were part of their family, and they saw to it that we were taken care of. I told them both that they had given us enough decorations that we would be able to decorate the house from the roof to the ground.

This goes back to why we bought the white Christmas tree. Well, first of all, I am a huge college football fan. My family is divided between teams, but none of us get rowdy with one another or anything. Instead, we find ways of having a good time together regardless of who wins or loses.

Anyway, my daughter and I had bet on the SEC Championship game, and I sort of kinda lost that bet. My children are LSU fans; I am an Alabama fan; and my dad is a Florida State fan, so now you can understand about my family being divided. Then I have very close friends who are Auburn fans, but we all get along wonderfully during and after football season. That is how true fans should be.

The bet was that if LSU won, then the kids could have an LSU-decorated Christmas tree and if Alabama won, then I could have my Alabama-decorated tree. Well, I lost and the kids got their tree. And just to throw this out there for good measures: Alabama and LSU met in the national championship game, and, well, I won't rub it in too much but, Roll Tide.

We do little family things like that. We enjoy the time we have together. By the way, everyone who came over to the house just loved the kids' Christmas tree and bragged on how pretty it was. So of course I had to explain the bet between me and Ro'chele because they would all ask where we came up with the idea for the tree. That was pretty funny, and she loved hearing me say that I lost.

We had a church organization that came through the valley and gave families brand-new pre-lit Christmas trees. They even had money donated to them to go out and buy Christmas gifts for the victims and their families.

When they came to our house, I was completely, as they say, lost for words. I was speechless. They had brought presents upon presents and food for us to have a Christmas. You talk about bringing tears to your eyes. Well, when I looked at who all they were from, it was miraculous. There were presents from young children who picked the things out themselves that they wanted to give. Talk about sharing the caring and loving season! They did just that.

We had one church that was on the other side at the end of the valley that had organized a foundation to help the victims as well. They had gotten together a group of Christmas carolers of all ages from their church who brought fruit by and sang Christmas songs to us. They also had brought a Christmas gift of money from the donations that they had received so we could have a Christmas and try to start back to having a solid foundation as we had moved back home.

That was so thoughtful and caring, and that was exactly what we all needed during the holidays—to be loved, to be showed that we were not alone and that people were there for us if we needed them. It made it so much easier for us to be able to sleep at night and not have to worry about where and how we were going to be able to give a few gifts to our children. Again, another God-sent gift of love to all of us.

The church of one of my dear friends and coworkers—actually, it was the same church that had painted the house—all came together and set aside money for us for after Christmas. They wanted to give us time to get moved in and settled in so we could see what else we might need.

We also had this other church organization that bought things for us after Christmas. Again, they wanted to give us time to get settled in and know what we needed. They had already bought me a gas grill and a deep freezer. Then they called me up after Christmas and said that they had more donations given to them for us and needed to know what else we needed to establish the house and make it home again.

I had begun to feel guilty at this point—guilty for all the help that we had been receiving. I told the young lady who called me from the church after Christmas that they had done so much for us that we didn't need anything else. God had provided us with a home, and they should use the money on another family.

She explained to me that I had no reason to feel guilty, that it was going to take a lot more than what I was thinking to get everything that we needed for the house. She also explained to me that all families were being taken care of by so many people all over the state that no one was going to be left out. She continued by telling me that God had provided plenty for everyone who needed help so I had no reason to feel guilty.

All these organizations that came together and churches from everywhere wanted each household to try to get back established just a little bit. And as long as God continued to provide and set on their hearts the families to help, they were going to continue doing their mission. I was so astonished and amazed that I could not stop crying. I was crying with joy, joy to know that so many people cared.

I ended up giving in to her and telling her a few things that I wanted for the house. I had met an elderly lady after the tornado who brought me a set of China dishes that I did not want to use, and they bought me a glass cabinet where I could put them on display for everyone to see.

Another dear friend of mine whom I had known for twenty-plus years attended the Church of Christ of Ashville. The Church of Christ churches all over the States were the ones that had organized and were bringing in so much food and different supplies for everyone all over the state. They were also able to provide to families brand-new washers, dryers, and refrigerators. It was wonderful.

All of these organizations and churches were not just helping Shoal Creek Valley victims but victims all over the state of Alabama. Shoal Creek Valley definitely needed the help because we were a small community. They made sure that we were not left out by any means.

Now before I go any further, yes, we had to make a little effort to make sure that we got on the list for help because we were victims and lost everything. But the people and organizations did everything that they could and some to help us. We, the victims, had to keep up with who was helping and who wasn't.

That was how a lot of us in the valley became close to one another; we were sharing information and helping each other in the best way that we all could. For most of us, we became a big community family, helping one another, so we could get through this together.

On April 27, 2012, people from everywhere observed the one-year anniversary. It was heartfelt for everyone. The observation for Ashville was held at the high school football field where it was called a celebration of hope. The stadiums were completely full. For the thirteen beautiful people we lost in our valley, they released a dove. There was not a person in the stadium who did not shed a tear, a tear of hope, a tear of love, and a tear for the will to strive forward.

Denise and her family and my family and I decided to get together that evening and have a one-year anniversary dinner and prayer. We had decided months before that we all ended up together for a reason. God had brought us to one another not only the night of the tornado but to also get through the trials that we had to go through to get back home. We decided then that God wanted us to stay together as a family, to continue helping one another and loving one another the way God intended us to do from the beginning of time.

Tony cooked for us and said the blessing at the same time as when the tornado swept through Shoal Creek Valley. We prayed for the families who had lost loved ones in the storm and gave praise to the Father for helping others. For we all had suffered in many different ways.

It didn't seem like it had been a year yet, but time flies by so fast. Our shelter hasn't been put in place yet, but Denise has one that is in the ground; we go over to her house if we have any bad weather as of today. We all still have fear that it will happen again, but considering what we went through, I know everyone understands why we take extra precaution.

Actually, Denise and I have this coordinating plan that the two of us do if the weather is supposed to be bad. After many nights of pacing back and forth and biting our nails, we decided to implement a buddy system. We take turns staying up and watching the weather, and we will either text or call the other to let the other person know what the weather is doing and if that doesn't work, she has a key to my house and I have a key to hers. This system helps both of us as far as keeping us calm during the storms.

Denise has really done a lot for me, helping me get through some tough issues that I didn't want to have to deal with but were beyond my control. She had to take me to the hospital one night with my arm because it had started swelling and turning red around the part the plate and screws were in. They ended up having to admit me in UAB Highlands and push antibiotics and morphine. The doctors said that I had extremely bad inflammation but no signs of infection under the plate. What had happened was I was trying to use my arm too much and I simply could not do the things that I was used to doing. Once again, my heart was hurt.

I had to see a series of different doctors on my post-traumatic stress, and I insisted on Denise going with me because she knew what I had been through as she has been there every second including the night of the tornado. I knew that if I broke down trying to answer questions, she could back me up and answer them for me. On top of that, we had become close friends and I just needed her there for support.

I had to see this one doctor who ran some pretty neat tests that told her some information on the trauma that she needed to know. She did memory tests, and that was how they discovered that I was blocking memory. They predicted within two years I would start remembering again. I'm not really sure that I want to. I have even noticed that there have been some people that I don't remember and it takes me a few minutes of talking with them to figure out who they are.

There are so many things that we take for granted in life that it's ridiculous. When it's too late, then it's too late. I learned that the hard way also. But I have also learned that it is important to live life properly and stay in touch with your closest friends because you may never see them again or, as in my case, have a problem with memory. But I have so many people who care, and they help me tremendously and are very patient with me. I love them so much. Just pure blessings from the good Lord from above.

Photos by Gary Hanner/St. Clair Times

Jeremv Cox presents Ro'chele Landry her trophy that was lost in the tornado.

My daughter's archery medal and trophy were found and returned to her after the tornado. Her archery coach, Coach Cox, presented it to her during the one-year anniversary ceremony that was held at the Ashville High School Football Stadium on April 27, 2012.

It took me a long time to be able to finally admit to myself that I couldn't get through this trauma as easily as I thought I could. I have always considered myself to be able to conquer just about anything, and I also have close friends who still to this day tell you that I will be okay and it won't take me long. But the truth is I could not go back and do the same things that I used to—like work, for example. There is no way that I would be able to jump in the car while on call to get to work in the middle of a storm again. I used to be fearless, and my main goal was to protect the water and public health. But I could not do those things anymore. I could not leave my children, and I know even if I was alone without anyone at the house, that I still couldn't force myself to do those things like I used to.

Every time a storm comes through, I can still hear the sound of that EF4 tornado. It's a sound that no one would be able to forget. I will never forget what it looked like. Those traumatic things really do hurt a person and change one's outlook on storms. Trust me. It did me. I was fearless, not afraid of anything, and would not hesitate at all. Now, it's different. I have to have comfort from others, and it's tough sometimes. One thing about me being able to admit my weakness is that I know it's a healing process, and in time, I may be healed, if not completely, then to a better degree than what I am now.

It takes a lot for a victim to become a survivor. The healing process isn't just physical but mental as well. I have come a very long way but only because of the people who have been there for me—to love me, to care for me, to listen to me when I needed someone to talk to and trust me, I have made a lot of very late phone calls to friends. But the ones who cared the most didn't care what time it was. They were always there, and that is how I became a survivor—with all of the help from others.

It wasn't just the older adults who helped make a way; it was the young adults as well. There was this one time that we were down at the property before any cleanup was being done, and I hadn't been out of the hospital long, and here came some of the kids that I knew from Ashville High School. Some had already graduated, and some were still in school. Football players, baseball players—they all came to lend a hand or a shoulder.

I couldn't help crying when I saw them all, because the known fact is that even though sometimes we have busy lives, we will always be there for one another. I saw that a lot from our little town of Ashville, Alabama. They all set aside their busy lives to be there for us in lending a helping hand and lending a shoulder to cry on. We cried, and they cried. It affected the whole town. That is the way it is supposed to be. You set aside any past feelings, and you make new ones by caring and being there for one another. That is exactly what Ashville did. We grew closer than we ever were before. Another one of God's plans: to bring people together, united as one.

I had to have another surgery on my arm in August 2012. All of my doctors had to coordinate with each other because of my medications. They had to go back in my arm and remove the plate and screws.

My arm would continue to swell and turn hot to the touch and fire red where the plate was. It had done this several times, and I either had to go to the hospital or doctor's office and have antibiotics because the only thing that would show up at the time was inflammation.

Then eventually, one orthopedic surgeon decided to run a

sonogram on my arm while the swelling wasn't so bad and found one possible problem that could have been causing the inflammation. I had a screw that had worked its way out and had shot through the other side of my wrist pinning ligaments, tendons, and nerves. The sonogram had actually showed that I had two tendons where there should have only been one, and that was because the screw had pushed it over to where it should not have been, causing problems. And that was where some of my pain was coming from.

None of the surgeons really wanted to have to remove the plate and screws because of the high risk that I possibly could have later with refractures. But they didn't have much choice either. They had to get that screw out of there.

Neither mentally nor physically was I ready to do this all over again—all the doctor visits, therapy sessions, and no driving. I had just started getting a little independence back. But it had to be done. We did all the paperwork and blood work at the same time I had the sonogram done so I wouldn't have to come back the following day to do all of my preoperating tests.

The surgery was a success. All the multiple fractures that I had looked good and were healing. I just had to be extremely careful. I was at higher risk for refracture now because I did not have the stability that I had from the plate.

I still cannot bear much weight at all on my arm. I was able to use the gadgets that Rhetta had made me to do therapy at home. The doctors figured that I had gotten as far as I would get with the previous therapy, and I was not able to do some of the things that I had done before in therapy right now anyway.

I do see a difference in not having the plate, and I often wonder if it wasn't a huge mistake removing it rather than just repairing the screw and leaving everything else as it was. I still have a lot of pain and swelling. My handwriting is awful now. That's something I'm just going to have to learn to live with.

I am definitely a weather-predicting person now more than ever. I can tell you when it's going to rain and when it's going to be cold. With my injuries, my body does not like that kind of weather.

My lower back locks up on me a lot because my S1 joint is shifted laterally to the left, and I refuse to let them wire it. So I deal with that pain as much as I can. My best friends during the moments of weather are a heating pad and many, many pillows to elevate my legs and arm and shoulder. I am sure, eventually, I am going to have to give in to a few more surgeries. But I am trying to deal with everything the best way I can. I have been through enough for a while. Lots of prayers. Lots of prayers.

To this day, I still find it remarkable remembering all of the people who came together for my state, my hometown, and my community. It gives me chills every time that I think about it, which is every day. I have had a lot of time to think about this whole devastating experience. And yes, I still find myself wandering around in the yard, looking for pieces of my past belongings.

What has killed my heart more than anything wasn't just the fact that we never found anything of my children's belongings, but I had some other very precious things that were dear to my heart that I never found.

My stepfather had passed away at a very young age due to cancer, and he was cremated by his choice. I never found anything similar to what I had his remains in. All of my great-grandmother's antiques and my grandmother's belongings that I had were gone. My nana's hand-crocheted items were gone. My baby rocker and my children's baby rockers were never found.

My house was full of old antiques and items that belonged to family members who had moved on to a greater place than here on earth. I had my grandmother's wedding ring set. I still had all of my high-school graduation things, including my class ring. I was so heartbroken at all of the material things that I had that would never be found. Not even a shred of wood.

My sister was able to find a few pictures that people had posted on websites when they had found people's belongings from the April tornadoes. She had actually found one of our vacation pictures from when we had gone on a cruise to Mexico.

Just a few of the locations where she found the pictures were Sand Rock, Alabama; Summerville, Georgia; Trion, Georgia; Flintstone, Georgia; and Rome, Georgia. Then there was one found in Centre, Alabama. That should give you an area picture of how big the debris ball must have been from the EF4 tornado, and that is why we never found anything that belonged to us here.

I had mentioned earlier that I have had a lot of time to think about the situation. I can't speak for anyone but myself, but I definitely took this devastating experience and developed a completely different outlook on the things in my life and my own personal opinion.

Remember, I continued to ask the question, "Why? God, why can't I find a shred of anything that belonged to me and my family?" When God saw that I was ready for the answer, this is what He told me. "Material things come and go. I gave you a memory to remember those things, but at the same time to get your attention, My child. You had greatly distanced yourself from me. Your antiques and material objects were more valuable to you than Me and my Son, Jesus Christ. This is the only way that I could bring you back closer to Me. You are My child, and I love you so much that I will go to great measures to protect you. I gave you a memory to remember those things. But you also must remember why I went through great measures to do what I have done."

Now, that's pretty powerful. It gave me a lot to think about. I started thinking about all the times my job was more important to me than anything else. I would always be the first to volunteer to work holidays and any given chance for overtime.

I basically had begun taking advantage of everything that God was giving to me and forgetting why He gave it to me to begin with. I had completely stopped thanking God for everything that He had done for me and my family. I had gotten used to the idea that, "Hey, it will be there when I get home." Nope, that wasn't the case as of 6:23 p.m. on April 27, 2011.

I feel like God was trying to get a lot of people's attention that day, not just the state, not just my valley, but the whole world. We continue to forget every day that He is in complete control of every obstacle course that we may encounter.

We sometimes forget what God's plan has been from the beginning and will continue to be to the end. I feel like we all must and will endure all types of tests and trials in life for a reason and it's to get our attention and make us really think about the matter. All God wants us to do is to love Him the same way that He loves us.

God took care of us after the tornado outbreak of April 27, 2011. He sent the people we all needed for help that evening to bring us together as a community and as a family. He helped us to set aside past troubles and to stop holding on to things of the past and move forward—to come together united as one.

We had all drifted apart. We were all too busy. We would only wave to one another on occasion, as we were passing by on the road either going home or going to work. Not only did we stop having time for one another but for God as well. He brought us together the way we needed to be brought together.

Whether people want to believe it or admit it, God did a miracle on April 27, 2011. For most of us, we watched it on television. Then there were the rest of us who directly witnessed and survived the EF4 tornado. I know that I lived through it to be able to talk about it and tell my story. It has been mental therapy for all of us.

My mission in life now is to get across to others that God is for us, not against us. He will do everything to take care of His children as He sees fit, not as we see fit and by no means on our time but in His time.

He sent wonderful, caring, and loving people from all over the place to help everyone. He wanted us all to reunite in the way that He planned it from the beginning, and He wants us to continue until the end. If God didn't love us, He would not have done the things that he has done. My family and I would not have a home, food, clothes, and the gift of experiencing what true love is all about.

I continue to stay in contact with everyone who has helped us, for the most part. There were so many people from all over the States that it was impossible to keep up with everyone. But I can say this: they all knew how much we appreciated and loved each one who came to help. I will never forget because God gave me a memory.

Denise and I are very close friends to this day. And every day we stay in contact with one another and visit each other at least once a day. I continue to be close to Tony and Gloria as well. They all may not realize it, but they gave me strength to continue moving forward. They are my family as well. Family sticks together in the worst of the worst storms, and we have done just that.

The recovery process will take many years. But with patience, it will all come together again. Some places may never get close to the way they were and looked before the tornadoes, but others may. We will all be reminded for a very long time of that day—especially as we ride down the valley. You can still see the tree lines where the tornado came in and left. But God will provide new growth.

It has taken me a very long time to accept some of the things that

I have had to accept. But I continue to give it all to God. Because God is why my family and I are here today. God showed me that He was "hope." And through Him anything can and will happen. But you have to let go of yourself and give Him everything.

It may not be always at the time you want it to happen, but God does have a plan. When He sees that you are ready, He will lead, guide, direct, and love you through your journey.

One last thing before I conclude this book. My friend, this is how I have gone from being a victim to a survivor: by God's word. And yes, He definitely kept His word, and now it's my turn.

Jeremiah 29:11 (NIV version):

"For I know the plans I have for you," declares the Lord, "plans to prosper you and not to harm you, plans to give you hope and a future."

About the Author

Stacy Michelle Landry is a freelance writer and author born in Pell City, Alabama, on April 1, 1971. Landry worked in the environmental business until April 27, 2011. In 1993, she moved her family to the beautiful countryside of Shoal Creek Valley in Ashville, Alabama. Her experience in the April 27, 2011, outbreak of devastating tornadoes in her community inspired her to write about the life-threatening events that she and her family survived. Landry and her children are survivors of an EF4 tornado that ripped through Shoal Creek Valley and came through the house that they were in, throwing them out into a field. Inspired by her true experiences, she wrote about the events of the tornado and the devastating aftermath in hopes of inspiring others to never give up. No matter what one may have to endure in life, one can go from being a victim to becoming a survivor. Based upon true breathtaking events, the author takes you step-by-step through everything that she experienced from having to leave her home behind and trying to seek shelter from the storm to having to figure out how to reestablish a new home. With the help of many volunteers and organizations, including several churches, she was able to set up foundations to rebuild her family home.

About the Book

This book is based upon the true story of the April 27, 2011, outbreak of tornadoes that came through the state of Alabama. An EF4 tornado swept through a community destroying everything in its path. But it did leave behind survivors to tell the story of that day. Experience the actual events one family did as they were being thrown out of a house and into a field and witness the determination by all and the people from everywhere coming to help the victims to live as they all a waited hours for medical help. Trees upon twisted trees and debris from everywhere all over the roads made it completely unrecognizable even to residents of the valley. Even though the injuries were major, people still fought to survive. They all kept their faith that help was not far behind. Relive the aftermath and the struggles as everyone in this community did. With a complete foundation of hope, faith, and love, people gathered from all over the States to come help.